The Ultimate Homemade Dog Food Recipe Book

Your 2 in 1 Guide and Cookbook to Healthy, Vet-Approved, Complete and Balanced Slow Cooker Meals with Daily Serving Guidelines

Ava Barkley

A Note to Readers

All information in this book, including text, pictures, and all other content, is intended for educational purposes only and should not replace professional veterinarian advice. We strongly encourage you to consult with your dog's veterinarian before making any changes to your pup's diet or healthcare routine. In emergencies or situations of concern regarding your pet, please seek immediate assistance from your veterinarian or local emergency veterinary clinic. Please note we are not endorsing any particular test, veterinarian, product, or concept that you may encounter while reading this book. Any decisions you make due to the information in this book are your own, and you take full responsibility. While we are here to provide you with information and insights, your pet's well-being is our top priority.

Illustrations

You might observe that our illustrations are primarily in black and white, a decision made to ensure affordability for our readers. Rest assured, the quality and depth of the content remain top-notch, aiming to provide comprehensive insights into your dog's nutrition. We are here to provide you with the help and support you need and appreciate your commitment to enhancing your dog's well-being. Together, as devoted dog parents, our shared mission is to ensure the long-term health and happiness of our dogs.

Exclusive Bonus: Homemade Dog Treat Recipe Book

Thank you for choosing this book as your ultimate guide to preparing homemade dog food! Your support has made this journey incredibly fulfilling.

As a token of my appreciation, I am thrilled to present an exclusive offer: **a FREE copy of my mini homemade dog treat recipe book**. This special bonus is filled with delightful treats that perfectly complement the complete and balanced meals featured in this book. Plus, it offers a sneak peek into my next publication.

To access your exclusive bonus, simply use your phone's camera to scan the QR code below or visit **www.avabarkley.com/freebook**

Scan me

Thank you again for your support. Here's to healthier, happier meals for our beloved dogs.

Ava Barkley

Contents

About the Author

MEET AVA BARKLEY, A devoted dog mom whose journey into homemade dog food began out of necessity, driven by her dog's health challenges. Confronted with this obstacle, Ava dedicated herself to extensive research and experimentation in canine nutrition and meal preparation. She collaborated with veterinarians to deepen her understanding and ensure her approaches were all-encompassing. Her efforts paid off, leading to a remarkable turnaround in her dog's health and vitality. This experience not only established Ava as the go-to expert in homemade dog nutrition among family and friends, but also as a trusted local authority for fellow dog owners seeking advice.

Her profound success in transforming her own dog's health ignited a passion to share her knowledge with a wider community. Ava's book on homemade dog food is the culmination of her detailed research and practical experience. It's more than just a guide; it's a reflection of her commitment to enhancing the lives of dogs through complete and balanced nutrition. In these pages, Ava shares insights, recipes, and tips to help dog owners embark on a journey towards a healthier, happier life for their beloved pets.

How to Read this Book

THIS BOOK IS A comprehensive guide and cookbook on homemade dog food, designed to cater to both novices and seasoned pet owners alike.

If you're new to the concept of homemade dog food, I recommend reading this book from start to finish. The book gradually builds upon the fundamentals of canine nutrition, guiding you through each step of transitioning your dog to home cooked meals.

If you already have some background in preparing homemade dog food, please jump to the sections that are most relevant to your current needs. The book is structured in a way that allows easy navigation to specific topics. Whether you're looking for complete and balanced recipes, detailed information on specific nutrients, or tips for managing dietary transitions and health issues, you can directly access these sections using the table of contents as a blueprint.

Happy reading, and here's to the health and happiness of your furry friend!

Introduction

I MAGINE STARING INTO THE hopeful eyes of your canine companion—those eyes that trust you to make the best choices for them. Diet, as many say for humans, is equally significant for our four-legged friends. It's the unseen force behind their wagging tails, their playful barks, and even their shiny coats. Nutrition is the backbone of their vitality and longevity.

But why veer toward homemade dog food in an era teeming with commercial options? Because, in every homemade meal, there's an unmatched assurance of freshness, quality, and genuine care. It gives you the freedom to know, choose, and decide what goes into that beloved bowl, ensuring every bite is as nutritious as it is delicious.

Enter Ava Barkley: a force to reckon with within the realm of canine nutrition. From a tender age, her life revolved around the dogs she adored. Her journey into homemade dog food began from necessity, driven by her dog's health challenges. Noticing the tangible link between her dog's diet and health, this curiosity turned into a lifelong quest. After extensive hands-on culinary experiments and collaborations with leading veterinarians and pet nutritionists, she not only improved the health and vitality of her dog, but also developed a holistic approach to canine nutrition that she wants to share.

In this book, Ava becomes your guide—your mentor. From deciphering your dog's individual nutritional needs to creating balanced, mouth-watering recipes, she's got your back. The transition to homemade might seem overwhelming, but with Ava's expertise, it'll soon seem like second nature.

Whether you're a newbie to homemade dog food or seeking deeper insights, this book promises clarity, knowledge, and above all, a healthier, happier pup. You will discover how to transition your dog to amazing complete and balanced homemade meals, monitor your dog's health, determine how much to feed your dog daily, and more! Together with Ava, embark on this enlightening journey and discover the transformative power of genuine nutrition for your furry friend.

Chapter One

Cracking the Code to Your Dog's Nutrition

E VERY BITE YOUR DOG takes impacts their health. But what truly makes a meal nutritious for them? Dive deep into the vibrant world of canine nutrition, where each little section holds a secret to your pup's radiant health and boundless energy. Ever wondered why the off-the-shelf kibble, no matter how *premium* it claims, doesn't resonate with your inner dog-parent intuition? Well, there's a delicious, wholesome world beyond that bag. Homemade dog food is not just a culinary choice; it's letting your four-legged friend know you care, promising flavors they've only wagged their tails in dreams about. This chapter? It's the gateway to a world of happiness with your pup, the beginning of a culinary adventure you and your dog won't forget. Let's unravel the magic together!

Your Dog's Microbiome

You have an incredibly resilient companion, one who enjoys excellent health, has a coat that glistens with vitality, and maintains a core strength that could impress even the most dedicated fitness enthusiasts! This is what good nutrition for your dog looks like. It's the secret that allows your pup to maintain a top-notch immune system, keep their skin and coat runway-ready, and ensure a healthy belly.

In fact, 80% to 90% of your dog's immune system is actually located in their gut, aka their digestive system (Pepin, n.d). This means that if you feed your buddy top-notch meals every day, you would strengthen their immune system, providing a long and healthy life! So many dog owners don't realize this and continue to roll the dice on store-bought kibble food.

The importance of your dog's diet extends to their gut health, where a complex network of bacteria, viruses, fungi, and other microorganism – known as the microbiome – plays a vital role in overall wellness. This microbial ecosystem aids digestion, absorbs nutrients, supports immune defenses, and even regulates key functions like hormone balance and vitamin production. However, factors such as stress, environmental chemicals, and, most importantly, poor dietary choices can disrupt this delicate balance, leading to chronic health issues.

Research has shown that feeding your dog a fresh, unprocessed diet rich in meats, fish, eggs, and vegetables can significantly improve their gut microbiome. Dogs on such diets enjoy better digestion, fewer allergies, and a reduced risk of chronic conditions like diabetes, high blood pressure, cancer, and other gastrointestinal concerns, such as irritable bowel syndrome and inflammatory bowel disease (IBS and IBD, respectively).

One of the most important bacteria found in your dog's gut is Fusobacterium, which thrives on fresh, meat-based diets. While antibiotics and processed foods can obliterate beneficial bacteria, a well-balanced, home-cooked diet can help restore these essential microbes, leading to better digestion and long-term health.

The good news is it's never too late to start! Changing your dog's food may not be the simplest thing in the world, but it will work wonders in helping your pet deal with their daily life. If you fill your dog's bowl with the appropriate food, you may improve their health in 80 percent of cases! So, what's the takeaway here? Make some dietary changes for your four-legged pal!

The Perfect Recipe for Your Pup

The food we offer our dog needs to have the appropriate amounts of protein, healthy fats (such as omega-3 and omega-6 fatty acids), carbohydrates, minerals, and vitamins, as well as an adequate quantity of water. Think of it as crafting the ultimate recipe for your buddy's well-being and finding that perfect, magical blend that will make your buddy the happiest pet at the park.

Should you find it challenging to recall the specific functions of each nutrient, remember that their roles in our dogs' health closely reflect their significance and purpose in human health.

Protein

Protein is a crucial component of a balanced diet, and the benefits of consuming protein go far beyond supporting muscle growth. It is necessary for the maintenance of cartilage, tendons, and ligaments, and also contributes to the health of skin, hair, and nails, in addition to the circulation of blood throughout the body.

Protein, in its simplest form, is a sophisticated structure created from a sequence of amino acids. This sequence is called the amino acid chain. Proteins are essential components of the skeletal framework of all living things, including humans and dogs. Proteins are responsible for various important structural functions. These functions range from the healing of cellular damage to the creation of essential enzymes and hormones that guide many physiological processes. One example of the latter function is the production of red blood cells.

The consumption of protein is of utmost significance for the domesticated dogs who share our homes. When we picture a dog playing fetch or sprinting through a park, the protein in the dog's food is hard at work, helping its muscles grow and repair themselves. Their playful energy and spirit partly stem from the protein-rich meals they consume.

Beyond muscle support, proteins introduce certain essential amino acids to a dog's diet. While our canine companions can naturally produce many amino acids, they must obtain some directly from their food. These indispensable amino acids are the hidden gems behind countless physiological operations, ensuring the body hums along smoothly.

Additionally, in times when fats or carbohydrates fall short, proteins step up as an alternative energy source, powering those tail wags and joyous leaps. But the wonders of protein don't stop there. It plays a silent, yet crucial role in bolstering the immune system. By aiding in the creation of antibodies, proteins stand guard, fending off potential illnesses and infections.

Lastly, for anyone who's ever marveled at a dog's glossy coat or admired the health of their skin, protein deserves some credit. A significant portion of a dog's skin and hair cells owe their existence to protein, making it indispensable for their outer glow as much as their inner vigor.

There are eleven essential amino acids that are important for dogs (Tupler, 2021):

- **Arginine**: This is essential for optimal kidney function and helps in the detoxification processes in dogs.

- **Histidine**: Crucial for growth and tissue repair, and aids in the production of red and white blood cells.

- **Isoleucine**: Helps support energy regulation, muscle recovery, and hemoglobin synthesis.

- **Leucine**: Promotes muscle growth and repair, while also helping regulate blood sugar levels.

- **Lysine**: Essential for calcium absorption and proper bone growth.

- **Methionine**: Assists in metabolizing fats and preventing fat buildup in the liver.

- **Phenylalanine**: Important for producing chemicals in the brain that regulate mood and pain signals.

- **Taurine**: Vital for healthy heart function, vision, and reproduction in dogs.

- **Threonine**: Supports a strong immune system by aiding in the production of antibodies.

- **Tryptophan**: A precursor to serotonin, it plays a role in regulating mood, appetite, and sleep.

- **Valine**: Supports muscle coordination, energy, and brain function.

When looking for high-quality animal protein sources, think of meats like chicken, turkey, beef, pork, lamb, bison, venison, and fish, such as sardines, salmon, or mackerel.

| BEEF | TURKEY | CHICKEN | LAMB |

| DUCK | PORK | FISH |

With the rise of plant-based diets for humans, are plant-based proteins good for dogs? Although dogs are most commonly thought of as carnivores, they have developed alongside humans and have adapted to efficiently absorb nutrients from plants. Some benefits of plant proteins for dogs include:

- **Digestibility**: Certain plant proteins are easier on a dog's digestive system, especially for those with sensitivities or allergies to specific meats.

- **Essential nutrients**: Plants often come with added bonuses, like vitamins, minerals, and fibers that are great for overall health.

- **Sustainability**: If you're environmentally conscious, incorporating plant proteins can reduce your dog's carbon "paw print."

Some fantastic plant protein sources include lentils, chickpeas, quinoa, and certain green veggies, like spinach, kale, green beans and broccoli.

Consider offering your dog a mix of both plant and animal protein sources to provide a well-rounded nutrient profile. Plant-based proteins are meant to be complementary to animal-based proteins, not a substitute as plant-based proteins do not provide enough or all the essential amino acids that dogs require. As always, consult with your vet to determine the best diet plan for your specific dog.

Fats

In terms of our personal eating habits, we tend to disapprove of fats, but for dogs, fats play a significant role in the diet. Consider them miniature energy factories. Compared to carbohydrates and proteins, fats provide more bang for the buck in terms of energy. Fats are not only a source of fuel, but also help the body absorb certain essential vitamins, including vitamins A and E. These vitamins are responsible for our puppies' picture-perfect, lustrous coats and their smooth, velvety skin. And let's not forget about the cognitive benefits, which are crucial for our exuberant puppies and our more senior dogs.

Nevertheless, it is not as simple as throwing any kind of fat into their dish. The sources are important. The fatty acids known as omega-3 and omega-6, found in fish oils and some seeds, are highly regarded for their beneficial effects on health.

But the fact is that maintaining a healthy equilibrium is essential. If your dog has too little, he or she won't enjoy the benefits. If you fill the bowl with an abundance of fats, you run the risk of your dog's health taking unexpected turns. A phrase I frequently use is, "everything in moderation."

Always keep a watchful eye on the source of the fats in the food that you provide your dog. In most cases, natural sources are superior. Egg yolks, sardines, chicken fat, hempseed oil, flaxseed oil, safflower oil, sesame oil, and krill oil are some excellent examples of nutritious sources of fats that may be given to your canine companion.

It is also key to know the different types of fats, as well as their unique benefits. Starting with Linoleic Acid (LA), an essential omega-6 fatty acid—it's primarily found in hempseed, and chicken, and pork fat. Now, omega-6 might sound technical, but in simple terms, these fatty acids generally contribute to your dog's growth, reproduction, and skin health. They play an indispensable role in maintaining the water barrier of the skin, ensuring it remains hydrated and healthy.

On the other hand, omega-3 fatty acids like DHA and EPA are renowned for the anti-inflammatory properties they possess, making them an invaluable tool in the fight against various health problems that our dogs may experience. Omega-3 fatty acids are sometimes referred to as the "superheroes" of the world of fatty acids, because they can treat many diseases and conditions, including dermatitis, arthritis, and certain types of cancer. Additionally, these fatty acids can be beneficial for our busy jumpers and runners, helping with potential cartilage problems or merely ensuring that our pups remain flexible and lively. The best places to get your omega-3s? Look for foods such as sardines, mackerel, salmon, and green-lipped mussels.

Omega-3 and omega-6 fatty acids each have their own advantages, but the way they interact makes them a truly magical combination. Omega-3 fatty acids, which are responsible for lowering inflammation and ensuring healthy joints, act as a counterbalance to omega-6 fatty acids, whose main function is to promote growth and skin health. It's almost like a perfectly choreographed ballet, each taking the lead when it's required to ensure our dogs get a nutritious diet that supports their overall well-being.

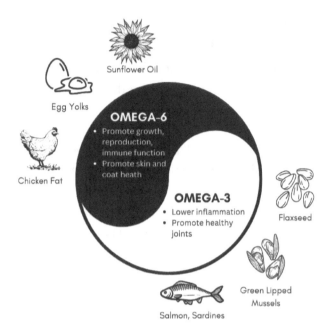

Always remember, like any dietary supplement, it's essential to strike the right balance between omega-3 and omega-6. Too much of one can overshadow the benefits of the other. And if you ever find yourself in a quandary about these fatty acids, a chat with your trusty vet nutritionist can put things into perspective.

Carbohydrates

Carbohydrates are considered another category of macronutrients, along with proteins and fats. Carbohydrates serve as a quick source of energy, and promote digestive health. It can be divided into two primary categories: simple carbohydrates, which include things like sugars, and complex carbohydrates, which include things like starches and fibers.

While dogs, in their evolutionary history, primarily consumed protein-rich diets, modern domesticated dogs have shown a notable ability to digest and utilize carbohydrates efficiently. However, it's essential to distinguish between different types of carbohydrates when considering your dog's nutrition. Not all carbs are created equal, and their effects on your pet's health can vary significantly.

What dogs don't need are refined carbohydrates, often found in commercial pet foods. These carbs convert quickly into sugars, which can trigger inflammation and lead to long-term health issues. For instance, a diet high in refined carbs can increase the likelihood of allergies and other inflammatory conditions as dogs age. Many dry pet foods contain up to 50 percent carbohydrates, which is far from ideal for maintaining your dog's optimal health. Thankfully, simply adding as little as 20 percent fresh, whole foods to their diet can help reduce these risks.

While dogs don't require refined starches, they do benefit from complex carbohydrates, particularly fiber. Fiber plays a crucial role in supporting a healthy gut microbiome, which is vital for overall health and digestion. These "good carbs" come from fiber-dense vegetables and fruits, which do not cause the sugar spikes associated with refined carbohydrates. There's a big metabolic difference between natural fiber-rich foods like broccoli and highly processed foods like white bread or pasta. Fresh, minimally processed produce provides not only the fiber dogs need but also essential antioxidants and phytonutrients that support long-term health.

In today's canine nutrition, the focus should be on incorporating these healthy, fiber-rich foods while limiting or avoiding processed carbs altogether. Some excellent sources of carbohydrates for our canine companions include green beans, butternut squash, apples, carrots, sweet potatoes, and pumpkin.

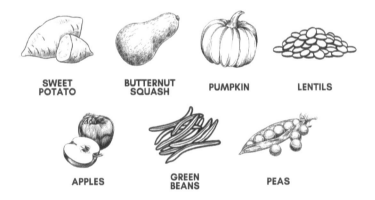

SWEET POTATO   BUTTERNUT SQUASH   PUMPKIN   LENTILS

APPLES   GREEN BEANS   PEAS

Vitamins

Vitamins are an important part of a healthy dog's diet, as they play a significant role in preserving a dog's health and warding off various illnesses. They were discovered around seventy-five years ago, and their significance resides in various tasks, including promoting cell development, preserving eye health, and assisting with the healing of wounds.

There are two categories of vitamins: water-soluble (like C and B-complex vitamins) and fat-soluble (vitamins A, D, E, and K). The fat-soluble vitamins need dietary fats for proper absorption and storage in the body. They can be stored in the body's fatty tissues, and excess accumulation can be toxic, necessitating careful dosage management. The types of vitamins include:

- **Vitamin A:** Vital for maintaining healthy skin, eyesight, and immune response in dogs. A deficiency could lead to skin lesions, poor coat quality, night blindness, and more susceptibility to infections.

- **B-complex vitamins:** Fuel metabolism, support the nervous system, and are tucked away in meats, eggs, and leafy greens. Most homemade dog food recipes out there are typically lacking in thiamine or vitamin B1, which is why you will notice nutritional yeast as a key ingredient in some of the complete and balanced recipes to come.

- **Vitamin C:** Unlike humans, dogs can synthesize their own vitamin C. But in times of stress, a little boost from food or supplements can be beneficial. Think of it as an antioxidant shield, warding off cellular invaders and damage.

- **Vitamin D:** Helps regulate calcium and phosphorus, critical for healthy bone formation and neuromuscular function. Insufficient vitamin D can lead to skeletal problems, heart disorders, and weakness. Over dosage is dangerous, causing calcium deposits in soft tissues and potentially leading to organ failure.

- **Vitamin E:** An antioxidant that protects cells from oxidative damage. Without enough vitamin E, dogs may suffer from muscle weakness, eye problems, and reproductive issues.

- **Vitamin K:** Needed for blood clotting. A lack of it can cause bleeding disorders.

Unlike fats, carbohydrates, and proteins, vitamins don't provide energy. However, they are necessary for certain physiological functions, and a dog's body can't produce them in adequate amounts on its own. As such, it is imperative they are part of the dietary intake.

Over or under-supplementation can cause health issues. Therefore, a balanced approach is needed. The natural content of these vitamins in food can be inconsistent, making supplementation a practical method to ensure dogs receive the right amount.

In summary, dog owners need to manage their pets' vitamin intake through a balanced diet to ensure their health and longevity. This responsibility means understanding the function and requirements of different vitamins, thereby preventing deficiencies or excesses, both of which can be harmful.

Minerals

Minerals are essential components of a dog's diet, because of the enormous influence they have on a dog's general health and the operations of their body. The health of the skin, coat, nerves, and bones, as well as the support of metabolic functions (such as digestion and the creation of blood cells), may be maintained with the help of these components, which are also engaged in various other physiological processes.

The two primary groups of minerals important for canines are macrominerals, which are required in large amounts in a dog's diet, and trace minerals, which are required in small amounts:

Macrominerals:

- **Calcium:** Vital for bone development, tooth formation, blood coagulation, and helping the heart and nerves function properly. An imbalance in a dog's calcium levels can lead to bone malformation or fracture, especially in growing puppies.

- **Phosphorus:** Works in tandem with calcium, promoting the formation of bones and teeth. It's also involved in the body's energy production. Too little can lead to stunted growth, while too much can inhibit the body's absorption of other essential minerals like iron and zinc.

- **Magnesium:** Necessary for protein synthesis, muscle and nerve function, stable heart rhythm, and a robust immune system. A deficiency in magnesium can lead to weakness, muscle tremors, or even seizures.

Trace Minerals:

- **Iron:** Essential for forming hemoglobin, the protein in red blood cells that carries oxygen throughout the body. Iron deficiency can cause anemia, which is characterized by weakness, fatigue, and increased susceptibility to infection.

- **Copper:** Supports the formation of red blood cells, aids in iron absorption, and helps maintain healthy bones, connective tissue, and immune function. It also plays a role in brain and heart health, making it essential for overall well-being.

- **Zinc:** Supports the immune system, cell growth, wound healing, and carbohydrate metabolism. Zinc deficiency can lead to hair loss, skin problems, and a weakened immune system.

- **Manganese:** Essential in a dog's diet for bone development, cartilage formation, and energy metabolism. It also acts as an antioxidant, supporting immune health.

- **Selenium:** Works as an antioxidant, protecting body cells from damage. It also supports thyroid function. Selenium deficiency can cause problems for the immune system and heart function, but an excess can be toxic, leading to issues like hair loss or even neurological damage.

- **Iodine:** Supports thyroid function, regulating metabolism, growth, and energy production.

It is essential to get the proportions of the minerals just correct. Any imbalance in the body, whether it be a deficiency or an excess (similar to vitamins), can lead to major health problems. For instance, a calcium-phosphorus ratio that isn't quite right might lead to bone issues in developing pups, such as rickets or osteoporosis in older dogs. Because of this, it is essential to strike the appropriate balance while preparing home-cooked meals for your dog.

Water

We all know that water is an essential nutrient for all living creatures, and your pup is no different. Any dog, especially active dogs, should consume 1 ounce of fluids (1/8 of a cup) per pound of body weight daily, since this is the standard rule of thumb for estimating the quantity of water a dog should drink. For instance, a dog that weighs 10 pounds should consume around 10 fluid ounces per day, while a dog that weighs 100 pounds should consume approximately 100 fluid ounces in a single day. Make sure you always have fresh, clean water available (Tupler, 2021 and Flower, 2022).

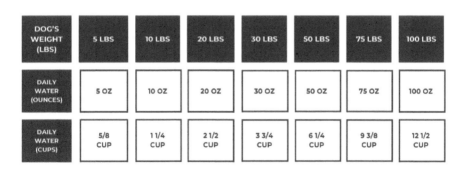

DOG'S WEIGHT (LBS)	5 LBS	10 LBS	20 LBS	30 LBS	50 LBS	75 LBS	100 LBS
DAILY WATER (OUNCES)	5 OZ	10 OZ	20 OZ	30 OZ	50 OZ	75 OZ	100 OZ
DAILY WATER (CUPS)	5/8 CUP	1 1/4 CUP	2 1/2 CUP	3 3/4 CUP	6 1/4 CUP	9 3/8 CUP	12 1/2 CUP

Consuming water and keeping it in the body are the two primary components of hydration, and ensuring that our dogs accomplish both is just as important for them as it is for us. Our canine companions require water not only to quench their thirst, but also because it is an essential component of their physiological health. Let's get into the specifics of why it's so important for dogs to drink water.

Firstly, water accounts for a considerable amount of a dog's body, perhaps between 60 and 80 percent. It is the fundamental constituent of each cell, tissue, and organ in the body. Every aspect of a dog's body, from the brain down to the bones, needs water to perform at its best. Other roles of water include:

- **Temperature regulation**: Dogs pant and rely on the evaporative cooling effect from their tongue, nasal passages, and lungs. This process helps them regulate body temperature, especially on warm days, and water is essential for this cooling mechanism.

- **Digestion and nutrient absorption**: Water helps break down food, allowing the absorption of nutrients that the body needs. It also plays a key role in metabolizing those nutrients to provide energy and keep organs functioning correctly.

- **Joint lubrication:** Proper hydration ensures that synovial fluid, which lubricates the joints, remains at its optimum consistency. This fluid makes movement smoother and less painful, especially important for senior dogs or those with joint issues.

- **Detoxification**: The kidneys play a pivotal role in filtering out waste and toxins from the bloodstream. Adequate water intake ensures these toxins are diluted and flushed out through urine, preventing potential kidney diseases and urinary tract infections.

- **Healthy skin and coat**: Well-hydrated skin is more resilient against external irritants, and it ensures your dog's coat remains lustrous and healthy.

- **Cellular functions:** At a microscopic level, every cell relies on water to function correctly. Cellular processes, from delivering oxygen to facilitating chemical reactions, depend on adequate hydration.

Remember that water isn't just a thirst-quencher for dogs, it's the lifeblood of their health and vitality. Keeping your furry friend well-hydrated ensures their well-being and happiness.

So how can you check for dehydration in your pup?

- Pinch the skin gently in the area located between your dog's shoulder blades.

- After that, carefully lift the skin, and then let it go.

- Observe how the skin reattaches itself to its proper position.

Your dog is well hydrated if the skin immediately returns to its previous position after being stretched. On the other hand, if the skin returns slowly or remains pushed up for a longer period, it's possible your dog is dehydrated. There are additional cautionary signals that should be considered, including:

- Gums that are dry, pallid, and tacky.

- Eyeballs that are dry and sunken in.

- A nose and mouth that feel parched (Mmaennche, 2021).

Water and proper hydration are just as important for your canine friend as their diet, vitamin, and mineral intake. Be sure to stay vigilant and always have water readily available for your pup!

Unlocking Kibble Mysteries

What if everything you thought you knew about your dog's kibble is only a small piece of a much larger puzzle?

Kibble that can be purchased in stores has several benefits, including convenience, portability, and less mess than homemade alternatives. Kibble is typically flavored with beef or chicken to encourage our canine companions to continue returning for more food. Kibble is made from processed meat, grains, and vegetables. On the other hand, it does not come without some drawbacks. The dry quality of kibble might provide digestive issues due to its low moisture level, and the carbohydrate dominance of kibble may not be suitable for less energetic puppies, which could contribute to unwelcome weight gain. The dry nature of kibble also makes it less likely that it will be digested completely. In addition, let's not gloss over the fact that some kinds of kibble might be plagued with less-than-stellar components, such as fillers, by-products, and various preservatives, that can cause skeptical pet owners to raise an eyebrow.

Now, kibble does stir up a mix of opinions among pet enthusiasts. Some swear by it, calling it the canine equivalent of a balanced meal, while others might turn up their noses, highlighting its processed nature. After all, shouldn't our dogs do the same if humans are steering away from processed foods? But here's the thing: dogs have unique nutritional needs. While kibble has its pros and cons, the final call hinges on an individual dog's needs, the owner's lifestyle, and what priorities shine brightest when it comes to feeding our loyal companions. Let's look at a general list together (Stratton, 2023 and Witter, 2021):

Here's why some pooches (and their owners) prefer kibble, in addition to some drawbacks.

BENEFITS	DRAWBACKS
HASSLE-FREE SERVING: Grab, pour, and done - no prep time needed.	**NOT ALL ARE TOP-TIER:** Like anything, some brands might skimp on quality, sneaking in fillers or less-than-stellar ingredients.
SHELF-STABLE: You can stock up without worrying about fridge space or quick expiration dates.	**THIRSTY FOOD:** Unlike its canned or fresh counterparts, kibble doesn't contribute to hydration.
LIGHT ON POCKET: Typically, kibble can be kinder to your wallet compared to some gourmet dog food options.	**ALLERGIES ALERT:** Keep an eye out for common culprits like grains or corn, which can be tricky for some sensitive stomachs.
BALANCED IN A BITE: Many brands have got the science down, packing essential nutrients into those tiny bites.	**LONG-TERM LOOPHOLES:** Stick to low-grade kibble for too long, and your fur baby might face issues, from packing on pounds to other health hiccups.
TAILORED TASTES: From pups with a few extra pounds to the seniors, there's likely a kibble blend made just for them.	**NEWS-WORTHY RECALLS:** No one likes seeing their dog's food brand in the headlines for the wrong reasons, but recalls, while rare, do happen.

So, is store-bought dried kibble truly detrimental to dogs? Knowing the contents of your dog's food is vital for their health. When opting for kibble, it's essential to be proficient in interpreting commercial food labels to distinguish between lower-quality options and the more nutritious ones.

Reading a commercial food label

Maneuvering the world of dog food labels can often seem like deciphering a complex code. With various regulations and marketing terminologies, it's crucial for pet parents to understand how to read these labels to ensure their furry companions receive nutritious and safe meals. Here are some practical tips for dog owners to consider when evaluating commercial dog food labels:

1. Scrutinize the first five ingredients:

Ingredients are listed by weight, with the heaviest ones appearing first. The initial five ingredients often make up the bulk of the food. Ideally protein, sourced from meat, should top the list, taking precedence over grains. Look for high-quality sources of protein (like "deboned chicken", "lamb" or "beef"), and avoid products where the list starts with "meat by-products", "meat meal" or fillers.

Note: Meat by-products are secondary products not intended for human consumption (like animal feet, organs, and heads). While they provide protein, they're generally considered less desirable than whole meats.

2. Assess the protein content:

High-quality dog foods typically have a substantial level of protein. Check the Guaranteed Analysis to see the percentage of protein in the food. Adult dog foods should generally have at least 18% protein, while puppy foods require around 22%.

3. Decipher the ingredient terminology:

Terms like "Chicken Dog Food" or "Beef for Dogs" imply the product consists of at least 95% chicken or beef. However, phrases with "dinner," "entree," or "platter" (like "Chicken Dinner for Dogs") only require 25% of the main ingredient.

The word "with" in the label (as in "Dog Food with Beef") indicates just 3% of beef is needed, and "beef flavor" means there's enough beef to give flavor, but no specific amount is required.

4. Be cautious with "natural" and "organic" claims:

These terms are often used for marketing. "Natural" may not always mean healthier, as it's not heavily regulated. "Organic" should imply that the ingredients are free from pesticides and artificial processes, but certification standards can vary, so it's worth verifying these claims.

5. Be cautious of filler ingredients:

Ingredients like corn, wheat, and soy are often used to bulk up dog food, offering less nutritious value. While some grains can be a good source of energy, avoid products that use these as primary ingredients, as they can be allergens and are less digestible for some dogs. If your dog is allergic to grains, there are grain-free options that incorporate alternatives like potatoes and legumes to ensure the diet aligns with your dog's specific health requirements and well-being. Aim to find a dog food with less than 20% carbs (and ideally 10%).

6. Check for by-products and specific sources:

If the ingredient list includes "meat meal" or "by-products," try to find a specific source (like "chicken meal" instead of just "meat meal"). While not all by-products are harmful, unspecified sources can be a red flag for lower-quality ingredients.

7. Understand AAFCO guidelines:

The Association of American Feed Control Officials (AAFCO) provides regulations for pet food, ensuring that products meet specific nutritional standards. The AAFCO seal on pet food brands acts as a reliable guide, and often references life stages (puppy/growth, adult maintenance, all life stages), helping you choose appropriate nutrition for your dog's age and activity level. However, senior dog nutrition requires a more discerning approach, as AAFCO's guidelines in this area are still evolving and waiting for more concrete standards (Wag, n.d.).

8. Consult AAFCO's definitions for clarity:

AAFCO has specific definitions for ingredients. Familiarize yourself with these terms to understand exactly what each ingredient means, and avoid vague or misleading labels.

9. Consider the nutritional adequacy statement:

This statement indicates whether the food provides complete and balanced nutrition. It will also tell you if the product is intended for a specific life stage, which helps select the right food for your pet.

10. Seek trusted brands and consult your vet:

Choose reputable brands known for their quality and safety standards. Reading online reviews and discussing with your veterinarian can guide you towards reliable options.

Navigating the complexities of commercial dog food options can often seem like a daunting task for dog owners. By becoming a savvy label reader, you're taking a crucial step in safeguarding your dog's health. Balanced nutrition is key to a happy, active life for your pet, and understanding what's in their food bowl is the first line of defense in their well-being (Cosgrove, 2023).

Yet, despite understanding commercial labels, many dog owners remain unconvinced that kibble is the right option, gravitating instead towards homemade dog food in their quest to provide fresh, quality meals they have full control over for their pets. By preparing your dog's meals at home, you can handpick high-quality ingredients, avoid unwanted additives, and customize recipes to suit your dog's specific health needs and preferences. Let's delve into why homemade dog food is gaining popularity, and how it could be a game-changer for your pet's well-being.

Why Consider Homemade Dog Food?

It is easy to feel overwhelmed when delving into the complexities of pet nutrition, especially in light of the growing trend of making homemade dog food. This method of canine nutrition has gained attention because of the possible health benefits it may offer, but it is essential for dog owners to have a comprehensive understanding of the situation. The following is a condensed and easy-to-understand explanation of the advantages and disadvantages of preparing homemade meals for your four-legged buddy, as well as some reasons you might want to give it some thought.

Advantages of homemade dog food

Healthier diet

Cooking your dog's meals at home allows you to use fresh, wholesome ingredients, cutting out the chemicals and fillers found in some commercial dog foods. This could lead to improved overall health, energy levels, and life expectancy for your pet.

Increased life expectancy

Scientific studies have illuminated the impressive correlation between diets rich in fresh, high-quality ingredients and increased life expectancy in dogs. For instance, canines thriving on meals made from freshly prepared, genuine food have been shown to live up to 13.1 years. This represents a significant 20% leap in longevity compared to those sustained on standard commercial pet foods, whose life expectancy hovers around 10.4 years, according to the Canine Bible (2022).

Tailored nutrition

Every dog is unique, and commercial food options don't always accommodate individual dietary needs. Preparing your pet's food allows customization in addressing allergies, dietary restrictions, and personal preferences, ensuring a well-balanced diet.

Easier digestion

Many dogs find homemade food easier to digest compared to some commercial kibbles according to a study from the University of Illinois (Quinn, 2019), which means better nutrient absorption and less strain on their systems. This is especially beneficial for dogs with sensitive stomachs or gastrointestinal issues.

Potential savings

While buying high-quality ingredients may initially seem more expensive, homemade dog food could save money in the long run. Healthier dogs are likely to mean fewer trips to the vet and lower vet bills, and buying ingredients in bulk can also reduce costs. Shopping wisely can help you make the most of your budget, especially when high-quality commercial dog food can be expensive, leaving pet owners looking for affordable options (Dog Child, 2023).

Allergy management

Embracing homemade dog food means more than just serving leftovers from your meals; it is about thoughtful preparation with dog-friendly ingredients. This approach is particularly useful for dogs with food sensitivities or allergies. By taking control of your dog's meal plan, you can identify ingredients that could trigger adverse reactions, allowing you to create meals that circumvent known allergens. This reduces irritation and improves your pet's quality of life.

Weight management and longevity

With the obesity epidemic in pets, controlling your dog's diet is more important than ever. Homemade diets allow for better control over calorie intake, helping prevent weight-related health issues and potentially extending your pet's life.

Challenges of homemade dog food

Nutritional balance

It's not just about throwing ingredients together. Dogs need a balanced diet, and without expertise in canine nutrition, it's easy to miss essential nutrients or provide an imbalanced diet that could harm your pet's health in the long run. Note: all the recipes in this book (see Chapter 6) are complete and balanced, fulfilling all nutrient requirements for a dog according to AAFCO guidelines.

Time investment

Undoubtedly, preparing meals at home is time-consuming. It involves planning, shopping for ingredients, and cooking, which might be difficult to fit into a busy schedule.

Storage issues

Homemade dog food doesn't have the preservatives that commercial foods do, meaning it can spoil more quickly. You'll need to be mindful of storage and use the prepared food within a suitable time frame to avoid wasting ingredients (see Chapter 5 for more information).

When preparing homemade food for pets, it is not enough to avoid the negative aspects. Instead, it is equally important to take advantage of the positive aspects. Understanding the components of a healthy canine diet and being prepared to spend time in the kitchen preparing meals that meet these requirements are necessary steps to commit to your pet's nutritional needs. What is the payoff? Your dog experiences the savory tastes, enticing fragrances and gratifying textures of fresh food that will make meals the most exciting part of their day.

In the end, preparing homemade meals for your dog is an investment in their health and happiness, potentially extending their life and undoubtedly enriching the quality of the years you spend together.

Understanding your dog's unique nutritional needs can be tough. It's become abundantly clear that dogs, much like humans, require a well-balanced and wholesome diet to thrive. In this chapter, we've explored the importance of proteins, fats, carbohydrates, vitamins, minerals, and water in their diet, unraveling the mystery behind what truly fuels your friend's health and vitality.

While kibble may be convenient, it often falls short of delivering the tailored nutrition dogs need. It is not a one-size-fits-all solution, as it is often marketed as. By now, you've learned the benefits of transitioning your canine companion to a diet that includes fresh, homemade meals.

In the next chapter, we'll guide you through the gradual transition to home-cooked meals, offering practical advice on how to avoid digestive issues, monitor your dog's health and identify common food allergies. So, as you embark on this journey toward healthier, happier days with your dog, remember that the path to their well-being lies in your hands and the choices you make in their diet.

Chapter Two

Kibble to Kitchen: Your Pup's Tasty Transition

M AKING THE SWITCH FROM store-bought kibble to home-prepared meals isn't something you'd want to rush when it comes to your dog's dining routine. Why, you may ask? Well, our canine companions have a way their digestive systems have grown accustomed to their regular chow, harmonizing everything from protein forms to fibrous components and the scale of fat contents. If we throw that off balance without warning, it's a recipe for tummy turmoil, marked by diarrhea, upset stomach, or even bouts of vomiting.

So, what does a gentle transition offer us? It is about giving the complex workings of your dog's gut the courtesy of time to acclimate to a new culinary landscape. Imagine the enzymes and the resident bacteria that need a grace period to quickly replenish and adapt to handle fresh, diverse ingredients efficiently. It is the kind of foresight that puts a lid on digestive mishaps and keeps adverse food reactions at bay when changing dietary gears.

Beyond the belly, we're also catering to our pups' palate preferences, which, believe it or not, can be as discerning as our own. Dogs harbor their food fondness, and a drastic change can send them into a tailspin of skepticism over their meals. Easing them into a new spectrum of flavors reduces mealtime anxiety and paves the way for a warm reception of the nutritious feasts you're whipping up.

In essence, this gradual shift is an exercise in mindfulness—a reflection of your commitment to improving your pet's well-being in a nurturing, gentle way. It's not a disruptive change in diet, but rather a thoughtful, loving transition that highlights the care we take to ensure our pets' overall health and culinary happiness.

Mastering the Art of Transitioning Your Dog's Diet

How to make the switch

It's imperative to exercise patience to ensure that our four-legged pals not only adjust, but thrive on a revised diet. Think of this transition as a gradual journey, rather than an abrupt switch. It is recommended to seamlessly blend the new food with the former over a period of two weeks to aid your dog's digestive tract in acclimating, ensuring the switch is both gentle and pleasant. If your dog has a sensitive stomach, choose a homemade recipe that uses a protein similar to the one in their current diet (if they are currently eating a chicken diet, choose one of the homemade chicken recipes in this book).

Here are some steps you can take to ensure this transition goes smoothly for both you and your pup:

- **Day 1-4:** Begin with 25% new food and 75% old food.

- **Day 5-10:** Move to an equal mix of 50% new and 50% old.

- **Day 11-14:** Shift to 75% new and 25% old.

- **Day 15:** Voila! It's time for the 100% new diet!

Below is a helpful chart with step-by-step instructions you can take to introduce new foods to your dog's diet:

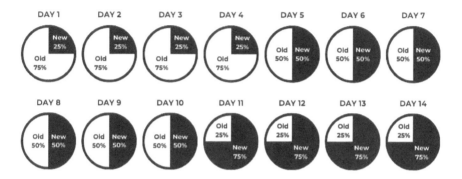

- **Step 1:** Take out fourteen empty containers and fill the first seven with the new diet at 100%, giving you your starting point.

- **Step 2:** Now, take 75% of the food from the first four containers and transfer it to the last four containers. This portions the new food for days 1-4 and 11-14.

- **Step 3:** Next, remove 50% of the food from the remaining three containers filled at 100%, and place it into the remaining three empty containers. This portions the new food for days 5-10.

- **Step 4:** To complete the process, simply fill all fourteen containers up to 100% with your dog's old food. Make sure to freeze the containers for Days 5-14, as cooked food lasts in the fridge for around 3-4 days.

Remember, some pups, especially those with sensitive tummies or dietary restrictions, might need an extended transition. The key is to keep a close eye on your furry friend's response. If they show signs of trouble, like appetite changes or tummy woes, slow down the transition. If issues persist, don't hesitate to consult your vet. They can offer guidance or recommend alternative diets tailored to your dog's needs, ensuring they thrive with every bite.

Dealing with picky eaters

Transitioning a picky dog to new food can feel frustrating. Here are a few helpful strategies for encouraging finicky eaters to try a new diet:

- **Start with Familiar Favorites:** Start with a protein and food/treat your pet is already used to. For example, if your dog likes beef-flavored canned food and soft beef treats, try offering similar options like home-made beef-based meals.

- **Avoid Free-Feeding:** If you tend to refill the food bowl throughout the day, remove it once your dog finishes eating. This helps them understand that food is available during set times, encouraging them to eat when it's offered.

- **Establish Meal Times:** Establish specific meal times and stick to them to create a routine for your pet. Note: a six-to eight-hour eating window supports your dog's digestive system and maximizes natural processes like detoxification. You can feed your dog one to two times within this window, ensuring your dog's daily calorie intake is met.

- **Monitor Portion Control:** Determine the right amount of calories your pet needs and stick to it. Overfeeding reduces the motivation for pets to try new foods.

- **Create a Calm Feeding Environment:** The location of your dog's feeding area, the level of activity around it, and even the height of the bowl can influence how they eat. Choose a quiet, low-traffic spot and consider using an elevated bowl to help them feel more comfortable during mealtime.

- **Make Gradual Changes:** Don't overwhelm your pet with too many changes at once. Whether it's the feeding time or the amount, modify only one variable at a time to monitor their response.

- **Be Patient and Persistent:** Reintroduce foods that were previously rejected. Dogs, like humans, can change their preferences over time. Offering a varied diet will help them adapt to new tastes as their needs evolve.

Sometimes, pickiness stems from habits unintentionally created by us. Offering table scraps can set higher expectations for tastier, more indulgent meals, causing your dog to reject regular food. Over time, this becomes a pattern where they anticipate—and even negotiate for—more flavorful options at mealtime. Our own food preferences can also complicate things, as dogs might develop a liking for the foods we eat, even though their nutritional needs are different from ours. Constantly switching their food in search of the "perfect meal" can reinforce this picky behavior, turning meals into a negotiation rather than a time for nourishment.

To break this cycle, follow the simple steps recommended by the Dog Nutritionist (Wimble, 2022):

1. Remove the food if your dog refuses it, then offer it again 15 minutes later.

2. If the food is still refused, cover it and store it in the fridge. Offer the same meal at the next feeding in about twelve hours.

3. Repeat these steps for the next three days.

While transitioning from commercial to home-cooked food may seem challenging, it is entirely possible with patience, consistency, and smart choices. Over time, your dog will adjust to the new diet and benefit from healthier eating habits. This process requires a little effort, but in the end, both you and your pup will find it worthwhile!

Monitoring Your Dog's Health

What your dog's poop reveals

After successfully making it through the process of changing your dog's diet, the next step in the journey is the most important: the painstaking process of ensuring your dog's continual health. This task needs a sharp, attentive eye toward both the overt physical indicators and the subtler behavioral adjustments. Casual observation is not sufficient to fulfill this obligation. Instead, it requires a keen, attentive eye. The consistency and quality of their stool is an important signal of canine health that is sometimes ignored.

Think of the stool your dog produces as a detailed health ledger—a thorough, albeit unorthodox, record of your pet's internal health. Your dog's excrement may tell you a lot.

It is essential you remember that you may see abnormalities during this period of adjustment. If you see any abnormalities or concerning shifts in the stool, you should take this as a sign to continue the new diet with the same mix ratio that you have been using. This is not necessarily an indicator that there is an issue with the food, but rather an indication of how quickly your dog is adjusting to the new diet. And if you find this voyage too difficult, there is no shame in turning around and going back the way you came. Whether that means returning to the old diet for a brief period or scaling back on the quantity of new food, the end aim is still the same: ensuring the wellness and contentment of your pet.

Although originally designed for human stool, the Bristol Stool Scale is a helpful tool to gauge your dog's digestion. This scale categorizes stools into seven types, ranging from hard lumps to liquid. Understanding where your dogs' stool falls on this scale can provide valuable information about their well-being (Wimble, 2022). The chart below can help identify what is healthy and what may be concerning. The 3-4 range indicated below is what is considered most ideal for the gut health of your dog.

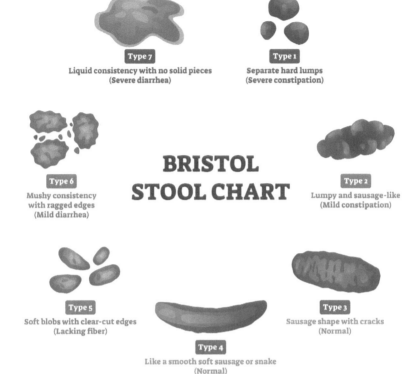

Image Credit: Shutterstock.com

Type 1 and 2:

These indicate constipation and may require dietary adjustments to increase fiber and decrease calcium intake.

Type 5, 6, and 7:

These suggest potential issues, such as a lack of fiber (Type 5) or inflammation (Type 6 and 7) (Wimble, 2022).

Additionally, the color of your pup's poop can also convey important messages about their health:

- **Dark Brown:** Healthy, caused by bilirubin from the breakdown of old red blood cells.

- **Black:** Can indicate gastrointestinal bleeding.

- **White:** May result from too much calcium or issues with the gallbladder, liver, or pancreas.

- **Green:** Could be due to plant-based foods or bile imbalances.

- **Red:** Often linked to certain foods or intestinal bleeding.

- **Orange:** From beta-carotene-rich foods or bile or bile duct blockages.

- **Yellow:** May signal fat-related problems.

In transitioning your dog's diet, your veterinarian is more than a guide—they're a vital partner in your pet's health journey. Strengthen this partnership by systematically monitoring your dog's progress. Keep a detailed log of weight, coat condition, energy levels, and behavior changes, with weekly weigh-ins as part of your routine. A dedicated journal offers valuable long-term insights.

While slight weight changes might seem minor, any significant shifts, especially with symptoms like vomiting or diarrhea, require immediate attention from your vet. Even stool frequency and odor provide clues—a balanced diet typically leads to two to three bowel movements per day, while an unusually strong odor or increased frequency may indicate underlying issues. These small observations contribute to your dog's overall well-being.

Understanding the ABCs of allergies and sensitivities

Understanding your dog's allergies and intolerances can feel overwhelming, especially if you're navigating these challenges for the first time. However, with a little patience and teamwork, we can work through these health puzzles together.

An allergy is a state of over-reactivity or hypersensitivity from the immune system to a particular substance called an allergen, which are proteins from plants, insects, animals or foods. Contrary to what some may think, food allergies in dogs may not necessarily manifest as gastrointestinal problems. Skin reactions are the most prevalent symptoms of food allergies in dogs, such as skin and ear issues. (Coates, 2020).

Venturing further, if we zoom in on skin allergies or dermatitis, a pattern emerges. Typically, these allergies find their roots in one of three primary antagonists: fleas, food allergies, or environmental irritants, also known as atopic allergies (AKC, 2021).

Types of allergies

	FLEA ALLERGY DERMATITIS	FOOD ALLERGIES*	ATOPIC ALLERGIES*
DESCRIPTION	• Triggered by flea bites or even flea saliva in some cases. • Manageable with targeted flea medications for dogs.	• Analogous to human food allergies. • True food allergies elicit an immune response.	• Dermatological problem that manifests as poor skin health. • Typically caused by seasonal and environmental factors, such as dust, pollen, mold and fungi.
TYPICAL SYMPTOMS	• Relentless itching, leading to redness, inflammation, and scabs.	• Gastrointestinal distress: diarrhea, potential vomiting. • Itchy ears or paw licking.	• Itching, with paws and ears being prime targets, which can lead to ear and foot infection. • Affected regions may also include wrists, ankles, muzzle, underarms, groin, eyes, and toe gaps.

*(Coates, 2020)

Symptoms of allergic reactions in dogs:

Allergic reactions can be classified into ear health, digestive symptoms, respiratory symptoms and skin issues.

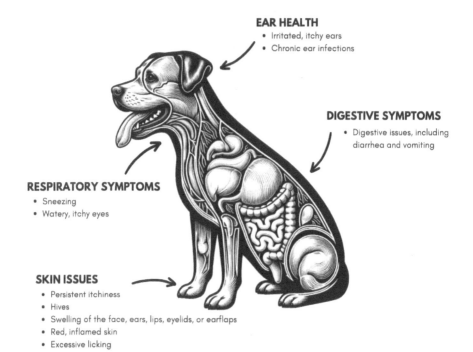

EAR HEALTH
- Irritated, itchy ears
- Chronic ear infections

DIGESTIVE SYMPTOMS
- Digestive issues, including diarrhea and vomiting

RESPIRATORY SYMPTOMS
- Sneezing
- Watery, itchy eyes

SKIN ISSUES
- Persistent itchiness
- Hives
- Swelling of the face, ears, lips, eyelids, or earflaps
- Red, inflamed skin
- Excessive licking

Types of allergens

Some proteins that often trigger canine sensitivities are—even if your pup has enjoyed these meats for years (Brahlek, 2022):

- Beef

- Chicken

- Eggs

Remarkably, beef and chicken are the most frequent offenders in causing issues for dogs.

Carbohydrates also pose challenges for many dogs, notably (Brahlek, 2022):

- Corn

- Wheat

Beyond proteins and carbohydrates, other ingredients can elicit sensitivities in dogs, such as (Brahlek, 2022):

- Dairy

- Soy

- Yeast

Please keep a close eye on your pup, especially if you think they might have an allergy or intolerance. Unchecked food allergies can lead to persistent itching, skin lesions, and in some cases self-inflicted harm, as dogs attempt to alleviate itching. Frequent ear infections are also associated with food allergies. These symptoms may resemble those triggered by environmental allergens, such as pollen, mold, and house mites (Coates, 2020). However, environmental allergies are often seasonal, while food allergies can be a year-round concern. Therefore, it's essential to monitor whether your dog's symptoms correlate with seasonal changes.

One pivotal revelation is that food allergies in dogs aren't necessarily static or predictable. Much like the ever-shifting sands of a desert, the landscape of a dog's immune response can evolve over time. This means that a food item, which your loyal companion has relished for years without the faintest hint of a problem, might suddenly become the trigger of an allergic reaction. The perplexing nature of these allergies doesn't end here. Imagine introducing a novel culinary delight into your dog's diet, and witnessing allergic symptoms manifesting almost immediately thereafter. It's a reminder of the unpredictability of immune responses and the need for vigilance.

Methods of allergy detection

So, how does one navigate this maze of potential allergens and decipher the root cause of a dog's allergic response? It requires a blend of detective acumen and an approach tailored to the unique needs of each dog.

The first step is to remove potential environmental triggers. Before looking at food as the culprit, consider taking away environmental factors that may be contributing to your dog's symptoms. Plug-ins, air fresheners, and household disinfectants can often trigger allergic reactions. Additionally, wiping your dog down after walks to remove potential outdoor allergens like pollen can help minimize irritants. Once you've addressed environmental factors, you can begin focusing on food-related allergies.

Consult your veterinarian for a precise diagnosis. Various tests are available to pinpoint the causative agents. With this knowledge, you and your vet can formulate a suitable dietary plan that aligns with your dog's physiology. (Klien, 2016).

At the heart of this investigative endeavor, two primary tools shine as beacons of hope.

1. Diet elimination:

Embarking on a journey to identify your furry companion's food sensitivities might seem daunting, but a methodical approach can make it an insightful experience. This strategy revolves around the concept of dietary simplification, a deliberate tactic to uncover hidden food triggers causing discomfort to your dog.

Starting anew with a single-protein diet:

Unlike humans, dogs can thrive on a monotonous diet for a short period. The process begins by removing your dog's current diet and introducing a single novel protein source—one your pet has never consumed before. Examples include venison, bison, fish, duck, rabbit, or kangaroo. This uniqueness minimizes the chances of pre-existing sensitivities interfering with the process.

Observation and detoxification period:

Maintain this minimalist diet for 2-3 weeks. During this time, your dog's system undergoes a sort of 'biological reset.' It's a detoxification interval, essential for eliminating lingering allergens from their body. Your pet isn't merely abstaining from certain foods; their body actively purges potential irritants.

Introduction and surveillance:

After the detox period, cautiously introduce another new protein or carbohydrate. It's vital to change only one food variable at a time to accurately detect any adverse reactions. You can also reintroduce old foods, and suspected culprits of the allergy. Monitor your pet's health and behavior closely during this phase, noting even subtle changes, be it their coat, energy levels, or stool consistency. Monitor your pet's progress as they adjust to the new diet. Improvement should be noticeable.

Detective work in action:

This process isn't just about elimination, but is an investigative operation. You're a detective, deciphering your pet's biological responses to different foods. Each new food component is a clue, helping you piece together the dietary puzzle to enhance your dog's well-being. Watch closely for any reactions, typically manifesting within days to weeks.

Consultation and customization:

Engage with your veterinarian throughout this process. Their guidance can help tailor the diet to meet your dog's nutritional needs, while avoiding triggers. Ultimately, this journey leads you to a custom dietary plan, contributing to a happier, more vibrant life for your four-legged friend.

Once you've identified the dietary triggers responsible for your dog's allergies, the next challenge is to avoid these problematic ingredients by following a few tips, such as:

- **Vet-prescribed fare:** Your vet can prescribe specialized allergy-friendly food tailored to your dog's needs.

- **Homemade goodness:** Take matters into your own hands by creating homemade meals from scratch, allowing total control over your pup's diet (see Chapter Six for recipes).

- **Limited ingredient diet:** Consider opting for a limited ingredient diet, simplifying mealtime to minimize potential allergens. Discover a selection of top-notch limited-ingredient dog foods tailored for allergy-prone pooches.

2. Food allergy blood test:

Sometimes, the subtleties of food allergies require a more clinical touch. In such instances, a food allergy blood test, administered by a veterinarian, emerges as an invaluable tool. By analyzing your dog's blood, this test seeks out specific antibodies produced in response to allergens, effectively spotlighting potential dietary culprits (Klien, 2016).

Armed with these effective strategies, you now possess the tools to pave a path toward an allergy-free, happy, and thriving canine companion. In the next chapter, we will delve deeper into nutritious foods and uncover key dietary choices that would benefit your pup, but also choices to keep away from.

Chapter Three

Nutritious Foods and Foods to Avoid

D OGS HAVE DISTINCT DIGESTIVE systems compared to humans. Certain food items acceptable for human consumption may actually pose a potential risk to dogs. Within the following chapter, a treasure trove of canine culinary wisdom awaits, designed to empower you as a discerning dog owner. Caring for our dogs goes beyond giving them food; it involves choosing the right nutrients to keep them lively and healthy. It's also up to us to shield them from foods that are okay for humans, but risky for pets.

This guide offers a deep dive into proper dog nutrition, showing how quality food can improve your pet's health and mood significantly. But it's not just about the good stuff. Some common foods around the house, like chocolate and grapes, are dangerous for dogs. These seemingly harmless snacks can cause serious health problems, from stomach issues to life-threatening poisoning. We'll list these dangerous foods to ensure they stay out of your pet's reach.

Nutritious Foods for Your Pup

Ensuring a balanced diet with nutritious foods for your dog is crucial for their health and energy. While dog food manufacturers do their part, they often don't include the fresh, wholesome ingredients every dog needs. That's where you come in! By introducing various beneficial foods, you can greatly enhance your pet's overall well-being. Below is a list of fantastic foods that you can start incorporating into your dog's diet.

- **Eggs:** These little protein powerhouses are perfect for your dog's muscles and ongoing tissue repair. The yolk is a great source of choline, supporting brain and liver function. Soft boiling or poaching eggs is the best cooking method, as it preserves the most nutrients compared to hard boiling, frying, or scrambling.

- **Blueberries:** These small fruits are big on benefits, offering antioxidants and essential fiber. This healthy treat supports cellular health and disease prevention.

- **Apples (without seeds):** Crunchy and full of fiber, they're a refreshing treat that also helps clean your dog's teeth. They contain vitamins A and C, beneficial for your pet's bones and immune system. However, the seeds and core should be avoided, as they can be harmful.

- **Sardines:** Packed with Omega-3s, sardines can enhance your dog's skin and coat, giving it a healthy shine. They're also an excellent source of protein, vitamins B12 and D, along with essential minerals like calcium and phosphorus, which support immune and bone health. Being low in mercury, sardines are a safe and nutritious choice. If opting for canned sardines, choose BPA-free cans and rinse them to remove excess salt. When preparing fresh sardines, be sure to remove the bones before serving.

- **Oysters:** Provide essential nutrients like zinc, iron, and vitamin B12. These nutrients support immune function, red blood cell production, and overall health.

- **Meats (such as beef, chicken, lamb, turkey, bison, venison):** These are essential for active dogs, providing the protein and amino acids they need for strong muscles and energy. Cook them well and serve them boneless.

- **Ground eggshell:** If your dog needs a calcium boost, ground eggshell can be added to their diet. It's excellent for strengthening bones and teeth. Organic eggs are preferable as it is believed some store-bought eggs are washed in a bleach solution which could be harmful to dogs.

- **Cooked veggies (like carrots, green beans, bell peppers, mushrooms):** These fiber-rich additions are great for your dog's digestive system. They add a nice variety to the diet, but they should be cooked without salt or seasonings.

- **Broccoli:** A great source of vitamins and fiber, that fights cancer and reduces inflammation and detoxifies the body.

- **Lettuce:** A great low-calorie snack and healthy training treat for overweight dogs, or those on a low-calorie diet.

- **Zucchini:** Dense in nutrients, it is a great source of vitamins and minerals, promoting a strong immune system, and healthy coat and skin.

- **Sweet potatoes and pumpkin:** These orange foods are fantastic for digestion and packed with essential nutrients, like vitamin A.

- **Butternut squash:** Full of vitamins A and C, potassium and fiber. It is exceptionally great for a dog's digestion, helping support a healthy immune system.

- **Plain yogurt:** A cool treat that's good for your dog's gut, thanks to its probiotics. However, make sure it's plain and doesn't contain any artificial sweeteners.

- **Natural peanut butter (free from xylitol):** Dogs love it, and it's a good source of protein and healthy fats. But stick to small amounts and ensure it doesn't contain xylitol, which is harmful to dogs.

Because the nutritional requirements of every dog are different, it is best to gradually introduce new foods and monitor any changes that may occur. Getting advice from your trusted veterinarian before making any changes is a good idea. They can direct you, depending on the particular dietary limitations and health requirements of your dog. Also, remember that your dog will benefit from adding these items to his diet, but each one alone is not intended to replace an entire meal (see Chapter 6 for complete and balanced meal recipes). The nutrition you provide for your dog is one of the most important factors in determining whether your dog will live a long and healthy life.

Foods to Avoid

For every dog owner, the welfare and vitality of their furry buddy is paramount. Part of safeguarding their well-being is understanding the dietary no-nos—those everyday foods that, while harmless to us, can pose a serious threat to our canine companions. Gaining insight into these dietary pitfalls is crucial to ensure they're well-fed.

Unlike humans, dogs metabolize food differently. A morsel that's a treat for you could be toxic to your pet, potentially causing anything from minor upset to severe health crises or even death. Dogs can be indiscriminate eaters, likely to ingest anything within reach, regardless of its potential harm. Hence, as a pet owner, it's imperative to be knowledgeable about which foods to steer clear of.

A rundown of no-go foods for dogs

Here's a brief look at various foods that spell trouble for dogs, along with the associated risks:

- **Grapes and raisins**: These can prompt acute kidney failure, with tell-tale signs including vomiting and a lack of energy.

- **Chocolate**: Laden with theobromine and caffeine can lead to health issues ranging from vomiting to seizures and death.

- **Allium family (onions, leeks, chives)**: These can irritate the gut and damage red blood cells, potentially causing anemia.

- **Xylitol**: Found in many sugar-free products, it can trigger an insulin spike, resulting in liver failure and a dangerous drop in blood sugar.

- **Alcohol**: Dogs are highly sensitive to alcohol, and even small quantities can cause severe intoxication, potentially leading to coma or death.

- **Caffeinated beverages:** Caffeine can be fatal, causing symptoms like restlessness, rapid breathing, and muscle tremors.

- **Cooked bones**: These can splinter, posing a choking hazard or causing internal damage.

- **Avocado**: The skin and pit contain high levels of persin, which could lead to vomiting and diarrhea. That being said, small amounts of avocado flesh are unlikely to cause problems given the concentration of persin is significantly less.

- **Macadamia nuts**: Known to cause weakness, vomiting, and fever.

- **Yeast dough**: It can rise within the stomach, causing bloating and potentially life-threatening stomach twisting.

- **Salty foods:** Excessive salt can lead to vomiting, seizures, and other serious health issues.

- **Garlic**: In large amounts, it can be more potent than onions as it carries the same anemia risk. However, some holistic vets believe garlic in small amounts can be beneficial.

- **Milk:** Many dogs are lactose intolerant and have difficulty digesting milk, leading to digestive woes. However, some lactose intolerant dogs can handle other dairy products like plain yogurt as it is typically easier to digest.

- **Corn on the cob**: While not toxic, it can lead to intestinal blockage.

GRAPES & RAISINS   CHOCOLATE   ONIONS, LEEKS & CHIVES   XYLITOL

MACADAMIA NUTS   COOKED BONES   CAFFEINATED BEVERAGES   MILK

Repercussions of ingesting dangerous foods can range from mild digestive issues to critical toxicity. Initial symptoms might include restlessness and vomiting, but these can escalate to dire conditions like seizures and organ failure.

Steps to take after accidental consumption

Act swiftly if your dog consumes something hazardous:

- Identify the ingested substance.

- Immediately reach out to your vet or an emergency clinic for guidance.

- Heed the vet's instructions, which might involve urgent medical intervention.

- To prevent repeats, ensure dangerous foods are inaccessible to your dog.

Being aware of harmful foods and knowing the correct course of action in case of accidental ingestion is pivotal in safeguarding your dog's health. When unsure about a food's safety, always seek your vet's advice. Remember, a well-informed pet parent is the best defense against dietary dangers.

Proactive steps to prevent accidental ingestion

- **Education is key**: Familiarize yourself and your family with the list of dangerous foods. It's not enough for only one person in the household to know; everyone should be aware.

- **Safe storage**: Keep harmful foods out of your dog's reach. This could mean storing them in higher cabinets or using childproof locks.

- **Trash management**: Dogs are notorious for rummaging through trash cans. Use cans with secure lids, and consider storing them in a place your dog can't access.

- **Be cautious with guests**: Guests might not know what's safe for dogs to eat. Inform them about your house rules regarding feeding your dog.

- **Mindful meal prep**: Be vigilant when preparing meals. Dogs can quickly snatch up any dropped pieces of food, so clean up spills immediately.

Regular vet check-ups

Routine vet visits are crucial for maintaining your dog's health. Your vet can provide personalized advice on what foods to avoid based on your dog's specific health needs, and can help you understand any breed-specific sensitivities.

Alternative treats

Instead of harmful human foods, opt for dog-safe treats (like freeze dried beef liver) and chews. These are specifically formulated to be both safe and appealing to dogs, and often come with additional health benefits, like dental cleaning or joint support.

Know the signs of distress

Even with all the precautions in place, accidents can happen. It's important to recognize the signs of distress that might indicate your dog has ingested something harmful. Symptoms can include:

- Vomiting or diarrhea

- Excessive drooling

- Coughing or gagging

- Changes in breathing

- Lethargy or weakness

- Changes in behavior or consciousness

- Seizures

Your dog relies on you for their well-being. By keeping harmful foods out of reach, educating those around you, and knowing what to do in an emergency, you're doing your part in ensuring your furry family member leads a safe, happy, and healthy life. Always remember that when in doubt, it's better to be cautious and consult with a professional. Your vigilance and proactive approach are the cornerstones of your dog's health and safety.

Chapter Four

Preparing Balanced and Healthy Meals

C RAFTING A WHOLESOME MEAL for your canine buddy is like curating a delectable dish for a cherished guest. It's a labor of love, a blend of science and art. In this chapter, we'll navigate this fascinating path together, ensuring that every bite your dog takes is not only nourishing and delicious but also complete and balanced. Every recipe in this book is formulated to meet your dog's nutritional needs, providing a well-rounded diet to support optimal health.

The foundation of any great meal lies in the quality and suitability of its ingredients. Our journey begins by selecting nutrient-rich ingredients and blending them for the perfect balance. Since standards are crucial—especially for those we cherish—we'll explore the Association of American Feed Control Officials (AAFCO) guidelines and highlight common nutrient gaps in homemade dog food recipes found online and even in most books. Every recipe in this book is designed to meet these top-tier nutritional standards, so you can trust that your furry friend is getting a meal that's not just tasty, but also nutritionally complete and balanced.

However, a menu's excellence isn't solely about its components, but also its portion sizes. In the realm of feeding our dogs, size matters, and knowing how much to feed your dog is equally important. Within these pages, we unravel the math and science behind portioning, ensuring your pet gets the right amount of sustenance tailored to their specific age, size, and activity level.

The Association of American Feed Control Officials (AAFCO)

Homemade dog food isn't just about mixing meat with grains and veggies. It's an intricate dance of nutrients, a balance that needs to be meticulously crafted and maintained for the long-term health and vitality of our dogs.

The AAFCO has laid down a blueprint for what constitutes a "complete and balanced" diet for dogs. These standards are not just mere guidelines, but the gold standard in pet nutrition. They ensure that every meal you prepare at home isn't lacking in essential nutrients. The AAFCO nutrient profiles provide a comprehensive list of the required nutrients for dogs, and the minimum and maximum amounts of each. They consider factors such as the life stage of the dog (puppy, adult, pregnant/lactating), and the dog's activity level.

For instance, proteins are the building blocks of a healthy canine body, fueling muscle growth and repair. Fats are a powerhouse of energy, supporting cell structure and promoting the absorption of certain vitamins. Carbohydrates, though not essential, serve as an additional energy source and aid digestion. Vitamins and minerals, though needed in smaller quantities, are pivotal in supporting physiological functions, from bone health to blood clotting, and antioxidant protection to oxygen transport.

Pet food companies look to AAFCO's standards as a golden checklist. If their food matches these standards, it means they're making quality food that's nutritious for dogs. It's like a chef making sure their recipe has all the right ingredients for a healthy and tasty meal.

AAFCO has created two main standards for dog food, called "nutrient profiles," and these depend on what stage of life your dog is in.

- **Adult maintenance:** This is for your everyday grown-up dog. These guidelines require at least 18% protein (like the meat in a meal) and 5.5% fat (like the oil in cooking), along with important minerals and vitamins to keep your dog healthy.

- **Growth and reproduction:** This one is for puppies who are still grow-ing and mama dogs who are pregnant or feeding their babies. They need more energy, so these guidelines bump up the protein to 22.5% and the fat to 8.5%, along with those important minerals and vitamins.

If dog food doesn't meet either of these guidelines, it's like a snack, not a full meal. It should only be given sometimes, not as the main food, because it doesn't have everything a dog needs to stay healthy.

13 Nutrients Commonly Missed in Homemade Dog Food Recipes

Most homemade dog food recipes, whether found online or in books, often lack essential nutrients and may not be nutritionally balanced. Nutritional deficien-cies can be hard to detect and may take a long time to show effects in your pet unless the deficiency is severe. Before feeding your dog a homemade recipe, it's important to ensure it contains the following 13 key nutrients to maintain your pup's health.

1. **Calcium:** Any homemade dog food recipe should include a source of calcium, whether from bone, bone meal, eggshell, or a supplement like calcium carbonate. If calcium is missing, avoid using the recipe. Long-term calcium deficiencies can weaken bones, lead to heart prob-lems, and cause muscle issues. Proper calcium levels, balanced with phosphorus, are crucial for your dog's health.

2. **Zinc:** It can be challenging to ensure sufficient zinc in a dog's diet, as organ meats like liver, kidney, and heart do not provide enough. For homemade diets, whole foods like oysters are excellent zinc sources. If a recipe lacks zinc or a supplement, it may be unbalanced. Zinc de-ficiencies can lead to digestive issues, poor skin health, slow wound healing, brittle coats, and in severe cases, heart problems, vision loss, and

blindness.

3. **Omega 3 to Omega 6 Ratio:** A good recipe should maintain a balance between omega-3 and omega-6 fatty acids. If a recipe contains only meat without added oils, it's a warning sign, as beef and chicken are high in omega-6s. To balance this, omega-3 sources like sardines, salmon, or flax seeds should be included. For fish-based recipes, adding omega-6-rich foods like chicken or pork fat is essential. An imbalance in omega-3 and omega-6 can cause chronic inflammation, worsening various diseases and conditions.

4. **Vitamin E:** This nutrient is often missing in homemade dog food unless specifically supplemented, as it's not abundant in meat or organs. If a recipe doesn't include vitamin E through supplements or sources like seeds, nuts, wheat germ oil, or dried oregano, it's likely deficient. Over time, vitamin E deficiencies can cause muscle weakness, paralysis, poor vision, and digestive issues.

5. **Manganese:** Good natural sources include mussels, cinnamon, cloves, and ginger. Muscle meats, organ meats, bones, and eggshells lack sufficient manganese to maintain overall health. Manganese is vital for joint and connective tissue health, and deficiencies can lead to conditions like ACL tears and metabolic issues, affecting blood sugar regulation, blood clotting, and nerve function.

6. **Vitamin D:** Dogs cannot obtain sufficient vitamin D from sunlight due to their fur, unlike humans. Therefore, they need to meet their vitamin D requirements through their diet. If a recipe lacks vitamin D supplements or organ meats like liver, it's likely deficient. Vitamin D deficiency can lead to skeletal problems, particularly in puppies, such as rickets, and can also cause immune system issues, cognitive impairment, and increase the risk of certain cancers.

7. **Iodine:** Iodine is difficult to find in most whole foods, as items like liver, kidney, heart, muscle meat, and produce don't contain adequate

amounts. In homemade dog food, kelp or seaweed are good sources of iodine. Otherwise, iodine supplementation is necessary to balance the recipe. Iodine deficiencies can lead to obesity, poor skin and coat (nutritional hypothyroidism), behavioral changes like anxiety and aggression, and weakened immune health, making dogs more prone to chronic infections.

8. **Copper:** When evaluating recipes, it's important to note that different organs vary in nutrient density. For example, copper is abundant in beef liver, but not chicken livers. If a recipe focuses only on poultry and lacks other organ meats like beef or lamb liver, pancreas, or spleen, it may be deficient in copper.

9. **Iron:** If you're feeding a poultry-only diet without supplementation, it's important to monitor iron intake. Iron is found in higher amounts in organs like spleen, heart, kidney, and beef liver. Recipes that rely solely on chicken livers are likely to be deficient in iron. A lack of iron can lead to anemia, causing symptoms like lethargy, shortness of breath, and reduced exercise tolerance.

10. **Selenium:** If a recipe lacks selenium supplementation and doesn't include oysters, mushrooms or kidney, it's likely deficient in this important mineral. Deficiencies in selenium can result in nail loss, skin and nail abnormalities, fatigue, a weakened immune system, and even hypothyroidism.

11. **Folate:** When evaluating homemade dog food recipes, ensure vegetation or supplements for folate are included, as it can be deficient in meat-only diets. Although some organ meats contain folate, the richest sources are plants like broccoli, kale, brussels sprouts and asparagus. Folate is crucial for DNA synthesis and red blood cell formation, and deficiencies can lead to anemia.

12. **Thiamine or Vitamin B1:** This nutrient is abundant in plant sources. Meat-heavy recipes that lack vegetation or supplementation may be

deficient in B1. Good sources of vitamin B1 include spinach, asparagus, and nutritional yeast. A deficiency in thiamine can lead to loss of appetite, nausea, and loose stools, which may progress to neurological issues and generalized weakness.

13. **Potassium:** If a recipe is composed only of meat, organ, and bone, potassium deficiency is a major concern. In homemade dog food, it's important to include plant-based potassium sources like spinach, mushrooms, parsley, beet greens, or chard. A lack of potassium can lead to muscle weakness, fatigue, nausea, cramps, bloating, and in severe cases, heart palpitations.

At the beginning of Chapter 6, we will delve into some key ingredients featured in the recipes in this book to ensure none of the essential nutrients are missing, providing your dog with a complete and balanced diet.

How to Structure Your Dog's Meals

Creating a well-balanced meal for a dog is like painting a masterpiece. It requires attention to detail, knowledge of the subject, and creativity. As we've explored in Chapter 1, a homemade dog diet should strike a delicate balance between proteins, fats and carbohydrates, while ensuring a complete and balanced meal with added vitamins and minerals. Let's delve deeper into the optimal ratios and roles of different food groups in a dog's diet.

The backbone of a dog's meal, which makes up 40-60%, should be muscle meat. This is where your dog gets proteins, the building blocks of life, and fats, which provide a source of energy that's more easily digestible for dogs. The beauty of muscle meat isn't just in its protein content; it's in the variety it brings to your dog's palate. Chicken, beef, pork, and turkey are all great sources, and they keep mealtime interesting for your furry friend.

Next, we have fish, contributing around 10% to a dog's diet. Fish isn't just a tasty treat; it's a powerhouse of fatty acids and omega-3, essential for a glossy coat and healthy skin. Moreover, these fatty acids support cognitive function and joint health, making fish a non-negotiable part of the diet.

But let's not forget organ meat, which accounts for 10-20% of the diet. If muscle meat is the backbone, then organ meat is the heart, loaded with vitamins and minerals. Organ meats can be divided into two categories: secreting organs and non-secreting organs. Secreting organs, like liver and kidney, produce essential hormones and enzymes and are rich in vitamins A, D, E, and iron. Non-secreting organs, such as heart and lungs, function more like muscle meats but still provide important nutrients like taurine and protein. Both types are crucial for creating a balanced, nutrient-dense diet for your dog.

Raw meaty bones, or their substitutes bone meal, should make up about 10% of the diet. They're not just there for fun; they provide essential calcium and help maintain dental health.

Fruits and vegetables, often overlooked, should comprise 10-20% of a dog's diet. They're not just fillers; they offer fiber, vitamins, and minerals that support overall health. Think of them as the canvas that holds the masterpiece together.

Carbohydrates should only make up ideally 10% of a dog's diet (up to a maximum of 20%). They're the frame of our masterpiece—supportive but not central. Healthier carbs, like cooked carrots, sweet potato and butternut squash, are preferable. Remember, while dogs can eat carbs, they don't need them as much as humans, and they don't digest them as easily. It's worth noting that the Association of American Feed Control Officials (AAFCO) doesn't specify a minimum requirement for carbohydrates, emphasizing their lesser importance.

Oils, though seemingly minor at 1-2%, are crucial. They're the finishing touches that add shine and detail, offering additional fatty acids and micronutrients that round off the meal. Examples of oils include fish oil, hempseed oil, coconut oil, olive oil, safflower oil, sesame oil, and krill oil.

Lastly, supplements such as vitamin D or E drops, at about 1%, are the varnish on our masterpiece. They ensure the meal is nutritionally complete, filling in any gaps that the primary ingredients might have missed (The Nutrition Guide, 2022).

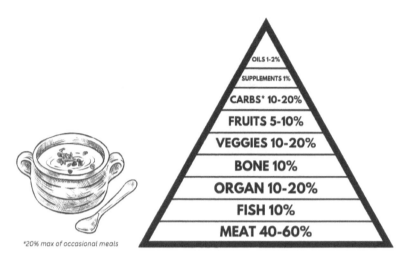

*20% max of occasional meals

Incorporating this knowledge into your dog's diet ensures each meal is a nutritional symphony, catering to your dog's needs in every bite. Remember, while dogs can metabolize carbohydrates, they thrive on a diet richer in proteins and fats. Carbohydrates, when included, should be carefully selected and limited to ensure they do not overshadow the more critical components of the meal.

Meeting Your Dog's Energy and Calorie Requirements

Feeding your dog is all about making sure they get enough energy from their food to match how much they move and live. Just like calories are a measure of energy for us, they are also for dogs. Determining daily energy requirements in calories dictates how much you need to feed your dog daily.

Each dog is different, with their own energy needs based on their age, whether they've been spayed or neutered, and how active they are. It's like being a chef who knows how to make a dish to keep the diners—in this case, your dog—feeling good and full of energy.

Determining the calorie requirements of your dog

Figuring out the exact amount of food to serve your furry friend each day can be quite the conundrum, like solving a puzzle with pieces that constantly change shape. Just like humans, every dog is a unique individual with dietary needs that fluctuate based on a medley of factors, including their weight, age, level of daily activity, and various life stages. This guide aims to take you by the hand and walk you through the maze of canine nutrition, equipping you with the knowledge to accurately calculate your dog's daily caloric intake and thereby portion sizes. We'll draw insights from authoritative sources and break down concepts like Resting Energy Requirement (RER) and Maintenance Energy Requirement (MER), complete with real-life examples.

The daily dietary needs of your canine companion are influenced by several core factors:

- **Weight**: The keystone in the arch of dietary needs, a dog's weight significantly dictates the amount of food they require. It's simple logic—more mass means more energy is needed to sustain it.

- **Age**: Puppies are like tiny bundles of boundless energy, undergoing rapid growth, thus demanding a calorically dense diet. Senior dogs, conversely, often have more sedentary lifestyles and slower metabolisms, necessitating fewer calories.

- **Activity level**: The more your dog moves, the more fuel they burn. Active dogs need a diet that keeps their energy tanks full, while couch potatoes require less to avoid unnecessary weight gain.

- **Life stage**: Just like different chapters in a book, each stage of a dog's life comes with its own nutritional script. Pregnancy, nursing, post-surgery, and even whether they're spayed or neutered, can dramatically alter their dietary script.

Feeding through the life stages

Navigating the nutritional complexities for our canine companions is paramount for their lifelong vitality and happiness. Each stage of a dog's life ushers in distinct dietary demands, much like the chapters in a book, each with its own narrative and necessities.

Puppies

Puppies, like energetic athletes in training, undergo rapid growth and require a nutrient-rich diet. High in calories and protein, essential for muscle and tissue development, their diet also needs vital vitamins and minerals, like calcium and phosphorus for bone growth, and omega-3 fatty acids for cognitive and eye health. Their caloric needs, often triple that of adult dogs, are best met with multiple small meals throughout the day to support their vigorous growth and vitality.

Adult dogs

As dogs mature into adulthood, their diet evolves from promoting rapid growth to maintaining a lean, healthy physique. Adult dogs need a balanced diet that provides enough energy for daily activities without leading to weight gain. Proteins remain crucial for muscle maintenance, fats for energy, and vitamins and minerals for essential nutrients. Their caloric intake should be carefully adjusted according to their size, breed, and activity level.

Expectant mothers

As a dog becomes pregnant, her nutritional needs increase. Initially, her diet may remain unchanged, but as the pregnancy progresses and the embryos grow, her calorie requirements will rise to support their development. Near the end of pregnancy, her food intake may double, depending on the expected litter size. A diet rich in high-quality proteins and fats is essential for the health of both the mother and her developing puppies. Regular veterinary check-ups are crucial to monitor her weight and adjust her diet as needed.

Nursing mothers

After giving birth, a mother dog's nutritional needs peak significantly. Caring for a litter is demanding, often requiring up to four times the usual calorie intake. Her diet during this phase should be protein and fat-rich to support ample milk production. Adequate hydration is also vital due to the high water usage in milk production, making constant access to fresh water essential.

Seniors

In their senior years, dogs experience a slower metabolism and reduced activity levels. They thrive on a diet lower in fats and higher in fiber for better digestion. Quality proteins are essential, but in moderate amounts to ease kidney function. Supplements, like glucosamine, chondroitin, and omega-3 fatty acids, are beneficial for joint and cognitive health. Regular vet visits are crucial to adjust their diet according to their evolving health needs.

The RER and MER: calculating caloric needs

In the realm of feeding your furry friend, two acronyms take center stage: RER and MER. These might sound like jargon, but they're pretty straightforward once you break them down.

- **RER**: Resting Energy Requirement

RER is like the basic subscription plan for your dog's energy needs—think of it as the baseline of your dog's diet. It's what your dog needs to lie around all day, do nothing but breathe, keep their heart beating, and basically stay alive. It doesn't include any extras, like going for walks, playing fetch, or even just wagging their tail.

- **MER**: Maintenance Energy Requirement

MER, on the other hand, is the premium package. It's the RER, plus all the extra activities your dog does throughout the day. Think of it as RER plus a day out in the park, running around, playing, and being an active dog. It also takes into account different life stages, like if they're growing puppies, pregnant, or nursing, because all these conditions require different amounts of energy.

Let's take a typical adult dog that weighs 10 kilograms (about 22 pounds) and loves to run around:

First, we calculate the RER, which is the energy needed if our dog did nothing all day:

$$\textbf{RER} = \textbf{70} \times \textbf{(Weight in kg)}^{\textbf{0.75}}$$

For our 10kg dog, it's:

$$RER = 70 \times (10\ kg)^{0.75} = 70 \times 5.62 \approx 394\ Calories/day$$

After calculating the Resting Energy Requirement (RER) for your dog, the next step is to adjust the calorie number to fit their lifestyle and specific conditions, which is where the Maintenance Energy Requirement (MER) comes into play.

Now, our dog isn't a couch potato. Let's say they're pretty active, so we adjust the RER to get the MER:

$$\textbf{MER} = \textbf{Activity Factor} \times \textbf{RER}$$

If the dog is active, the activity factor could be 1.8, so:

$$MER = 1.8 \times 394 \approx 709\ Calories/day$$

This is the total amount of calories this 10kg dog needs to consume daily to support all its activities.

Here's a guide to understanding how to adjust the RER based on a dog's individual lifestyle and life stage. Each of these multipliers reflects the additional energy your dog needs beyond just resting.

Adult spayed/neutered dogs:

- If your dog has been spayed or neutered, they typically require fewer calories due to a slower metabolism. Therefore, multiply the RER by 1.6 to find their MER.

Adult intact (not spayed/neutered) dogs:

- Intact dogs generally have a higher energy requirement. Multiply the RER by 1.8 to calculate their MER.

Pregnant females:

- During pregnancy, a female dog's calorie needs gradually increase. In the early stages, you may multiply the RER by 1.6, but as pregnancy progresses, this may increase up to two times the RER.

Nursing mothers:

- Nursing mothers have the highest energy demand, especially when they have large litters. Their MER can range from two to six times the RER, depending on the number of puppies and stage of lactation.

Puppies:

- Young puppies up to four months old require a lot of energy to support their rapid growth and development. The MER can range from two to three times the RER. As they grow, you will need to adjust their food intake accordingly.

- ○ A puppy aged four months to adult = 2.0 x RER

- ○ A puppy zero to four months = 3.0 x RER.

Seniors:

- Older dogs, or seniors, often need fewer calories if they lead a less active lifestyle. Start with an RER multiplied by 1.6, then adjust based on their activity level and medical conditions.

The calculations for Resting Energy Requirement (RER) and Maintenance Energy Requirement (MER) are valuable tools to help you gauge how much to feed your dog. However, it's important to remember that these numbers serve as a starting point. Each dog is an individual, with unique needs that may not be fully captured by a formula.

Understanding RER and MER can help ensure you're feeding your dog the right amount of food for their individual needs, keeping them healthy and happy!

Getting the measurements right

Just like a finely tuned instrument produces the most beautiful music, your dog's diet needs that same level of precision to ensure they thrive.

When it comes to feeding your dog, getting the amount right is key, and it all starts with knowing their exact weight. This isn't about a rough guess; you need the precise number to figure out how much food they need. This is because the calories your dog needs to lounge around—their RER—depend directly on their weight. To calculate your dog's RER correctly, an accurate measure of their weight is non-negotiable. You wouldn't guess the amount of flour needed to bake a cake, right? Similarly, guessing your dog's weight could lead to over or underfeeding.

But it's not just about hitting the right weight on the scale. Regularly monitoring your dog's body condition gives you a clear picture of their overall health. Is their waist well-defined? Can you feel their ribs without a thick layer of fat? These observations are the high notes that indicate your dog's diet is on point.

If you notice a change—perhaps they're looking a bit rounder or leaner than before—it's a sign to adjust their calorie intake. The goal is to keep your dog's weight in harmony with their size and breed standards, ensuring that every calorie consumed contributes to their vitality and zest for life.

By keeping a close eye on your dog's weight and body condition, you can orchestrate their diet to perfection, ensuring they remain healthy, active, and happy. It's not just about feeding your dog; it's about crafting a nutrition plan that resonates with their very being. So, let's embrace this responsibility with the dedication it deserves, and make every meal a stepping stone to optimal health.

This process involves assessing your dog's weight and conducting a visual and tactile examination, known as body condition scoring.

First, you will need to know your dog's weight to accurately calculate their RER. Here's a method to weigh your dog using a standard home scale:

- Start by stepping onto the scale alone to determine your weight.

- Gently lift your dog and step back onto the scale while holding them.

- Subtract your weight from the combined weight to reveal your dog's weight.

- For tiny breeds, consider using a baby scale to simplify the process.

Body Condition Scoring (BCS)

Body condition scoring allows you to visually and through touch evaluate your dog's health status. It is a hands-on check to see if your dog is too thin or carrying extra pounds. Here's a simple guide:

- **Rib check**: The ribs should be discernible, but not prominently protruding. Place your hands on your dog's rib cage; the ribs should be palpable with a slight layer of fat, not hidden under a thick cushion.

- **Profile and overhead checks**: Observe your dog's profile from the side and above. A tucked-up abdomen from the side and a defined waist from above indicate a well-proportioned physique, much like the elegant contours of a well-crafted violin.

Identifying weight categories

Armed with the knowledge of your dog's weight and body condition, you can tailor their diet and exercise routine to ensure they stay in optimal shape. If they're underweight, consider increasing their calorie intake. If they're overweight, it might be time to cut back on the treats and increase their activity. For those at an ideal weight, maintain your current regimen to keep them in harmony.

- **Underweight**: If your dog's ribs, spine, and pelvic bones are prominently visible, with minimal fat coverage and an obvious abdominal tuck, it's like an instrument with strings too tight—it indicates your dog is underweight.

- **Ideal weight**: When the ribs are palpable with minimal fat coverage, the waist is discernible when viewed from above, and the abdomen is tucked up when viewed from the side, your dog is hitting all the right notes—this is the ideal weight.

- **Overweight**: If the ribs are difficult to feel under a heavy layer of fat, the waist is barely visible or absent, and the abdomen sags, it's like an instrument out of tune—your dog is overweight.

UNDERWEIGHT	IDEAL WEIGHT	OVERWEIGHT
• Ribs, spine and pelvic bones are prominent	• Ribs, spine and pelvic bones are discernible with a slight layer of fat on top	• Ribs difficult to feel and under a heavy layer of fat
• Minimal fat coverage on ribs	• Abdomen is tucked up	• Waist is barely visible or absent
• Pronounced abdominal tuck	• Waist is visible when viewed from above	• Abdomen sags

It is also important to adapt your multipliers to the weight goals of your canine companion.

- **Total daily calorie intake required for weight loss of a dog** = *1.0 x the RER of the ideal weight of the dog.*

- **Total daily calorie intake required for weight gain of a dog** = *1.2-1.8 x the RER of the ideal weight of the dog* (Primovic, 2015).

Regular monitoring of your dog's weight and body condition is vital to ensure you are feeding the correct amount of food. It's a proactive approach that allows you to make informed decisions about their diet and exercise, ensuring they remain healthy and vibrant—much like a well-tuned orchestra delivering a flawless performance.

Not all calories are equal

Crafting a feeding plan for your furry companion goes beyond filling their dish. It's like personalizing a human diet. Let's delve into the nuances:

- **Grasping caloric richness**: Foods vary in caloric content. Richer, fatty foods have more calories than leaner choices. This means if your dog's diet includes more of these rich foods, they won't need as much quantity wise to satisfy their daily calorie needs.

- **Tailoring meal sizes**: Knowing your dog's caloric necessity, adjust their meal sizes based on their food's caloric density. This could mean less of a high-calorie food or more of a low-calorie one. It's the energy value in the food, not just the volume, that matters.

- **Source of calories matter**: The source of the calories is as important as the quantity. Calories from whole, nutrient-rich foods will support your dog's health much better than those from processed or sugary treats. Opt for high-quality meals and healthy treats that contribute to their overall well-being.

- **Regulating treats to manage calories:** Treats can sneak in extra calories. They should stay under 10% of your dog's daily calorie intake. If you've treated your dog to snacks, subtract those calories from their meal portions to keep their diet balanced.

It is also essential to note the importance of measuring your dog's food properly with a food scale. This will ensure that you accurately measure the calories you are putting into each meal for your dog.

In short, think of yourself as your dog's personal nutritionist. Structure their meals appropriately, keep track of their weight, watch their body shape, and adjust their meals as needed. It's all about making sure your dog gets the right amount and type of food for the energy they use every day.

Chapter Five

Sourcing, Prepping, and Storing Homemade Meals

T HIS CHAPTER WILL TAKE you on a culinary journey that feeds not just your dog's body, but also their soul. You'll learn how to source the freshest, healthiest ingredients to create meals that will have your dog's tail wagging with every bite. Next, we'll dive into the heart of the kitchen, where you'll discover the essential tools to make meal prep quick and effortless.

Of course, no chef can succeed without mastering food safety. You'll pick up crucial tips on proper food handling and cooking to keep meals safe and free from harmful bacteria. Plus, bulk food prep will be your best friend on busy days—imagine a freezer stocked with ready-to-heat meals that lock in flavor and freshness.

We'll also cover common pitfalls to avoid, from creating imbalanced meals to improper portioning, ensuring your homemade dog food journey is smooth and rewarding. So, roll up your sleeves and let's cook like gourmet dog chefs! Your dog's path to health starts in the kitchen, and we're here to guide you every step of the way.

A Guide to Sourcing the Right Food

As you curate your pantry with ingredients, prioritize freshness and purity. Envision each protein, each grain, and each vegetable as a key ingredient to the masterful dish that will keep your dog thriving. Whether it's lean cuts from the local butcher, or the ripest vegetables from the market, each choice is a testament to your commitment to their well-being.

Protein is the cornerstone of your dog's diet, and when it comes to choosing the right kind, variety is key. While chicken breast and ground beef are staples, organ meats, like lamb, beef or duck livers, pack a nutritional punch. These items might not be on the shelves of your local supermarket, but don't fret.

Venture into ethnic markets in your area. These gems are not just cultural experiences, but also offer a broader selection of meats, often at better prices. Whether it's a bustling Asian market or a vibrant Mexican bodega, you're likely to find those sought-after organ meats that provide essential nutrients for your dog.

If your local market draws a blank, consider a trip to the farmer's market. Here, local farmers may not have organ meats on display, but a simple conversation could lead to a fruitful arrangement. Often, they have surplus organs from butchering that are not commonly sold, and might be willing to sell them to you at a reasonable cost.

Another avenue is to join forces with fellow pet parents through a raw food co-op. Such communities purchase directly from suppliers in bulk, which means savings for everyone involved. However, be prepared for bulk buying, which might mean you'll need extra freezer space to store your bounty.

When it comes to fruits and veggies, seasonality can affect availability. But there's a solution: the freezer aisle. Frozen produce is picked and frozen at peak ripeness, locking in nutrients. They're a fantastic out-of-season alternative, often more affordable and just as healthy as their fresh counterparts. Just be vigilant about reading labels to avoid any added sugars or seasonings.

For those elusive items that are truly seasonal, consider stocking up during their peak season and freezing them yourself. This way, you're prepared year-round, and your dog won't have to miss their nutritional benefits (Giovanelli, 2022).

Kitchen Tools for a Canine-Friendly Kitchen

To create nutritious and delicious meals for your dog, it's important to have the right tools in your kitchen. Here's a list of must-have essentials:

- **Food scale:** A must for precise measurements in dog nutrition. Eyeballing portions is unreliable. Ensure the scale measures weight in both grams and ounces.

- **Cutting board and sharp knives:** Necessary for efficiently chopping meats and dicing vegetables into dog-friendly sizes.

- **Slow cooker / Crock-Pot:** Ideal for gently cooking complete and balanced meals, and broths.

- **Baking dish:** Useful for baking egg shells for egg shell powder, or dog treats, adding variety to the diet.

- **Grater:** Handy for quickly shredding vegetables, especially for dogs needing extra fiber or to hide veggies in their meals.

- **Large mixing bowl:** Essential for mixing ingredients before cooking or storage.

- **Food processor:** A key tool for picky eaters, as it blends vegetables finely, making them less noticeable.

- **Storage containers/Tupperware:** Important for safely storing prepared dog meals, with adequate freezer and fridge space needed. Choose glass containers, as they are less likely to harbor harmful bacteria compared to other materials like plastic. They are also free from harmful chemicals and do not release toxins into food.

FOOD SCALE   CUTTING BOARD   POTS & SLOW   FOOD PROCESSOR
              & KNIVES   COOKER

GRATER   MIXING BOWL   BAKING DISH   STORAGE
                                        CONTAINERS

Armed with the right tools and practices, you're not just making meals; you're ensuring your dog's health and happiness, one bowl at a time. So, go ahead—be the gourmet chef your dog thinks you are!

Food Safety

Transforming your kitchen into a sanctuary of safety for your dog is equally crucial. Foods that spell delight for humans can often be hazards for our canine friends. Keep those chocolates, onions, grapes, and other no-nos in high places or behind secure cabinet doors. A trash can with a robust lid is also a must-have to deter any curious noses.

And, of course, good hygiene is paramount. Always wash your hands and clean surfaces before and after preparing your dog's food. Keep their feeding and food prep areas clean. Utensils and bowls should be washed in a dishwasher or with very hot water—at least 155 degrees F (68.3 degrees C) to kill any lurking bacteria. This, along with proper cooking, is your best defense against food-borne illnesses, ensuring your pet's food is as safe and healthy as possible.

With your kitchen transformed into a fortress of nutritional value and safety, you're not just feeding your dog; you're lovingly crafting each meal with intention and care. It's this proactive approach that will keep your beloved pet's health on a joyful, wagging journey.

Meal Prepping Tips, Bulk Food, and Storage

Tailored food prep techniques

When preparing homemade meals for your dog, there are four main ways to handle ingredient prep, each catering to your dog's specific preferences, dietary needs, and chewing abilities. Here's a breakdown of these different preparation methods:

1. **Coarsely Chopped:** This method involves roughly cutting ingredients into larger chunks. Coarsely chopped food is great for larger dogs that enjoy chewing and prefer a bit more texture in their meals. Meats, vegetables, and fruits can be chopped into bite-sized pieces, providing a hearty, satisfying meal that encourages chewing.

2. **Finely Chopped:** Finely chopping ingredients into smaller pieces is ideal for dogs that prefer smaller bites but still enjoy a bit of texture. It also helps to mix ingredients more evenly throughout the dish, ensuring that each bite provides a balanced array of nutrients. Finely chopping is particularly useful for dogs that are picky eaters or have smaller mouths.

3. **Minced:** Mincing food involves cutting ingredients into very small, uniform pieces. This method is helpful for pets with smaller mouths, older dogs with dental issues, or picky eaters who may prefer smoother textures. Mincing also makes it easier to mix ingredients together, ensuring your dog gets an even distribution of nutrients in every bite.

4. **Pureed:** For dogs that have difficulty chewing or digesting, pureeing ingredients is the best option. Pureed food provides a smooth consistency that's easy to eat and digest, especially for older dogs or pets with dental issues. This method also ensures that the flavors and nutrients of the ingredients are fully blended, making the meal palatable and nutritious for even the pickiest eaters.

These different preparation methods allow you to tailor your dog's meals based on their individual preferences and health needs, ensuring they enjoy their food while receiving all the essential nutrients.

Diving into bulk preparation

Starting with smaller batches is a smart move when you're new to the homemade dog food scene. It gives you the chance to see how well your dog takes to the new diet before you commit to making larger quantities. Plus, it allows you to try a variety of different recipes according to your dog's taste and nutritional needs, without wasting food.

Once you've found the meals that make your pup's tail wag with joy, it's time to scale up. Batch cooking weekly or monthly can be a game changer. You'll want to set aside a few hours for cooking, but think about the free time you'll have during the week when mealtime rolls around, and all you need to do is serve (Giovanelli, 2022). A food processor can be a godsend, capable of chopping or blending ingredients with the push of a button.

Storing your culinary creations

Now, let's talk storage. Freshly cooked dog food can stay fresh in the fridge for about three days. If you've cooked enough to feed an army of pups, the freezer will be your best friend, keeping the food good for up to a month to avoid nutrient losses over time. Whether refrigerating or freezing, airtight containers or vacuum sealed bags are the way to go. They keep the food fresh and prevent unwanted freezer burns or fridge odors from seeping in.

Glass containers are excellent airtight containers —they don't harbor smells, are easy to clean, and you can quickly check what's inside. If you prefer plastic, make sure it's BPA-free. Labeling each container with the date of preparation helps you keep track of freshness and ensure your dog is only eating the best.

When freezing, consider portion sizes. Freezing individual meal portions or daily portions makes life easier—you won't have to thaw more food than needed. Silicone molds or cupcake trays are perfect for freezing single servings. Once frozen, pop them out and store them in your airtight containers or freezer bags (Giovanelli, 2022).

Recap on proper food storage:

- Use airtight containers or vacuum sealed bags to keep food fresh and prevent odors.

- Store in the fridge for short term (up to 3 days) and the freezer for long term (up to a month).

- Use glass containers or BPA-free plastic for health and safety.

- Label everything with the prep date.

- Freeze in portions to make thawing and serving straightforward.

- Thaw safely in the fridge, not at room temperature or in the microwave.

- Maintain cleanliness throughout the entire prep and storage process.

Thawing and serving

Thawing the food correctly is just as important as how you freeze it. Transfer the next day's meal from the freezer to the fridge the night before, letting it thaw gradually and safely. Avoid microwaving to thaw, as this can cook the food further and reduce its nutritional value. Room temperature thawing is not recommended, as it can encourage bacterial growth. If your pet prefers their food gently warmed, you can use a hot water bath to heat it. Simply place the container of thawed food into a larger bowl or container filled with hot water, allowing the food to warm evenly without cooking it.

By following these steps, you'll have a well-oiled meal prep machine that ensures your dog is eating healthy and making the most of your precious time. Remember, feeding your dog is more than just a daily chore—it's an act of love that contributes to their long-term well-being. With your new meal prep and storage strategies, you're all set to serve up health and happiness in a bowl (Giovanelli, 2022).

Common Mistakes to Avoid

Embarking on the journey of preparing homemade meals for your dog is a rewarding experience, but it's essential to be mindful of potential pitfalls to ensure optimal health.

Crafting a nutrient-rich meal

Creating a balanced diet is more than combining protein with greens; it's about ensuring every essential nutrient is present (as discussed in Chapter 4), like a well-composed symphony.

Stick to the recipe

Modifying recipes without guidance can lead to an unbalanced diet, so it's crucial to follow them closely or consult a nutrition expert when making changes.

Ingredient selection

Selecting the right ingredients is vital. While some foods, like chocolate or onions, are safe for humans, they can be harmful to dogs. Always ensure that your kitchen is free from these hazards.

Mastering the cooking process

Cooking for dogs requires precision. Undercooked food may carry bacteria, while overcooked meals lose nutrients. Find the perfect balance for proper nutrition.

Portion precision

Guesswork in portioning meals can lead to weight or health problems. Use a reliable food scale to ensure your dog gets the right amount for their size and activity level and utilize our daily meal portioning charts that accompanies each recipe in Chapter 6.

Avoiding common pitfalls

Introduce new foods gradually, monitor hydration, and always provide fresh water. Transitioning to homemade food should be done with expert advice to ensure your dog's dietary needs are met.

By mastering these aspects, you'll create meals that not only nourish your dog but enhance their overall health, ensuring each bite contributes to a happier, healthier life.

<u>Exclusive Bonus:</u> Homemade Dog Treat Recipe Book

If you haven't already, don't forget to download your exclusive offer: **a FREE copy of my mini homemade dog treat recipe book**. This special bonus is filled with delightful treats that perfectly complement the complete and balanced meals featured in this book. Plus, it offers a sneak peek into my next publication.

To access your exclusive bonus, simply use your phone's camera to scan the QR code below or visit **www.avabarkley.com/freebook**

Scan me

Thank you again for your support. Here's to healthier, happier meals for our beloved dogs.

Ava Barkley

Message from Ava Barkley

Thank you so much for reading this far! If this book has brought any value to you and your dog's life, I would be deeply honored if you could spare a moment to share your thoughts with a review on Amazon.

I personally read every review posted as your feedback is incredibly important to me. It helps me understand what resonated with you, and what could be improved to serve you and your dogs in my next book!

To leave a review, simply scan the QR code below (that matches the country you are in) with your phone camera to be taken to the book's review page.

If you prefer, you can also leave a review by:

1. Visiting the book's page on Amazon or locating it through your purchases.

2. Scrolling down to the bottom of the page and clicking on the "Write a Customer Review" button.

3. Leaving a star rating out of 5, or if you're feeling inspired, writing a short review to share your experience.

Thank you once again for your incredible support. It means the world to me and the countless dogs whose lives we're improving together.

Chapter Six

Complete and Balanced Recipes

W ELCOME TO A CURATED collection of nutritious recipes crafted especially for your beloved canine companion. This chapter unveils a comprehensive array of high protein and low-carb recipes tailored to meet the diverse dietary needs of dogs. Each recipe is meticulously detailed with macronutrient profiles, caloric content and portion sizing charts, empowering you to make well-informed decisions about your dog's diet. As a bonus, we've carefully included options for dogs with food intolerances that includes novel proteins like bison, venison, and rabbit. For busy pet owners, you'll discover straightforward, time-saving recipes ideal for bulk cooking and freezing, ensuring your dog enjoys a nutritious and appetizing meal even on your most hectic days.

When you adhere to the full recipe guidelines, these recipes meet the complete and balanced dietary standards for adult dogs as set by The Association of American Feed Control Officials (AAFCO). Always consult with your veterinarian before transitioning your dog's diet to ensure suitability for their individual lifestyle and nutritional needs.

What Sets our Recipes Apart

Unlike many homemade dog food recipes that fall short nutritionally, every recipe in this book has been rigorously crafted to meet the AAFCO's strict standards for complete and balanced nutrition. The formulation software used to develop these recipes is the Animal Diet Formulator (ADF), which integrates USDA data and verified international food information to create a robust nutritional database of ingredients. This tool is developed in collaboration with veterinarians, board-certified veterinary nutritionists, pet food manufacturers, and other industry experts, ensuring adherence to the latest FEDIAF and AAFCO guidelines. After extensive research and refining hundreds of recipes, I've selected only the best—recipes that are not only flavorful but also nutritionally complete. Every meal is designed to provide optimal health benefits, ensuring your dog enjoys every bite while thriving on superior nutrition.

The motivation for creating these recipes came from an unsettling discovery: an overwhelming majority—95%—of dog food recipes available in popular books and online fail to provide a complete and balanced diet, often lacking essential nutrients. An in-depth review of hundreds of these recipes revealed that about 83% had multiple nutritional shortfalls, frequently missing vital nutrients such as Vitamin D, Vitamin E, Zinc, Calcium, Copper, Choline, Riboflavin, Thiamine, and Vitamin B12, which are imperative for preventing long-term health problems.

Realizing the gaps in homemade dog food recipes prompted me to ensure all recipes in this book adhere strictly to nutritional guidelines, ensuring there are no nutritional shortfalls. This book represents my commitment to elevating canine nutrition. A meticulously balanced diet can pave the way for a robust immune system, a lustrous coat, and a life filled with vigor and longevity.

Call-outs on Specific Ingredients

You might be curious about why certain ingredients are used in multiple recipes, or how we made our specific selections. These ingredients are carefully chosen to ensure your dog receives complete and balanced nutrition, ensuring the right combination of essential vitamins, minerals, and nutrients are present in these meals and to guard against deficiencies. Specifically:

- **Kelp Powder:** Rich in essential vitamins and minerals, especially iodine, which supports thyroid function and metabolism. It also improves skin, coat, immune health, and digestion. The iodine content in kelp powder can vary greatly, so it's important to choose a brand that specifies 700 micrograms of iodine per gram of kelp powder.

- **Oysters:** Included to fulfill the zinc, iron and vitamin B12 requirements that support immune function, skin health, and overall well-being. You can easily find canned oysters packed in water at most grocery stores. *If you'd prefer to substitute with a zinc supplement, 1 ounce (about 28 grams) of oysters provides approximately 10 milligrams of zinc.*

- **Nutritional Yeast:** A great source of Thiamine (also known as vitamin B1), supports energy, brain function, immune health, and a healthy coat. It also adds flavor to homemade dog food, making it more appetizing. *If you'd prefer to substitute with a thiamine supplement, 1 ounce (about 28 grams) of nutritional yeast provides approximately 20 milligrams of thiamine (vitamin B1 supplement).*

- **Turmeric:** Rich in curcumin, it provides anti-inflammatory and antioxidant benefits, supporting joint health, digestion, and immune function. It's a valuable addition to homemade dog food, especially for dogs with inflammation or joint issues.

- **Egg Yolk:** A rich source of choline, which is a crucial nutrient for a dog's cognitive function. Choline plays a key role in supporting brain health, liver function, and nervous system development.

- **Egg Shell Powder:** A natural, easily absorbable source of calcium, crucial for balancing the phosphorus in meat-heavy homemade dog diets. It supports bone health, muscle function, and prevents calcium deficiencies that can lead to weakened bones and other issues.

- **Cinnamon:** Offers anti-inflammatory and antioxidant benefits, aids in blood sugar regulation, supports heart health, improves digestion, and freshens breath. It's a valuable addition to homemade dog food, especially for dogs with metabolic or inflammatory conditions.

- **Hempseed Oil:** Rich in Omega-3 and Omega-6 fatty acids, it promotes healthy skin, coat, joints, and supports immune and heart health.

- **Vitamin D:** Regulates calcium and phosphorus levels, which are essential for maintaining healthy bones and teeth. Since dogs cannot produce sufficient vitamin D from sunlight alone, it must be included in their diet. Without adequate vitamin D, dogs can develop bone disorders.

- **Vitamin E:** Vital in a dog's diet as an antioxidant that supports immune health, skin, coat, and cardiovascular function. It aids fat metabolism and protects cells, with deficiencies potentially causing muscle weakness and immune issues.

Cooking Considerations and Tips

Let's roll up our sleeves and dive into the nitty-gritty of cooking some scrumptious homemade dog food. It's not just about tossing a few ingredients into a pot. There's an art to it, and I'm here to guide you step by step.

Cooking methods

When preparing the recipes in this book, you have flexibility in how you cook them, depending on your goals and preferences for your dog. You can choose to serve the food raw, poach it on the stovetop, gently cook it using a Crock-Pot or slow cooker, or as a mix of raw and gently cooked.

- **Raw:** If you prefer to serve raw food, it can be done entirely without cooking. This is an option for those who want to retain all the natural enzymes and nutrients. However, if you have concerns about potential parasites in raw meats, freezing them for at least three weeks can help reduce the risk of harmful pathogens. You can also choose to feed only the vegetables raw and combine it with gently cooked meats.

- **Gently Cooked:** Gently cooking dog food is an excellent method for preserving nutrients and preventing nutrient loss. Unlike high-heat cooking methods like baking or frying, which can break down essential vitamins and minerals, slow cooking gently heats food over time, maintaining nutrient integrity and retaining important enzymes and fatty acids. This approach ensures your dog enjoys a nutritionally complete meal that's also moist, flavorful, and easily digestible. There are two ways to gently cook a recipe:

  - **Poached on Stovetop:** Prepare the recipe as directed and add it to a large pan, cover with filtered water, and a lid to prevent moisture and nutrient loss. Cook over low heat until the food reaches an internal temperature of 165°F. This method creates a soft, tender meal, ideal for dogs who may need a gentler food texture. Any associated cooking liquid must be included and served with the cooked food.

  - **Slow Cooker / Crock-Pot:** Using a slow cooker is another way to gently cook meals. Add the ingredients, set the cooker to low heat with no water added, and cook to the desired doneness. This method retains more nutrients while ensuring that the food is cooked evenly and thoroughly. Any associated cooking liquid must be included and served with the cooked food.

Cooked weight vs. raw weight ingredients

When measuring ingredients for these recipes, it's important to pay attention to whether the ingredient must be weighed cooked or raw. If cooked, weigh your ingredients after cooking, as the cooking process can either reduce or increase their water content, affecting the final weight.

As a general rule of thumb, meats, poultry, seafood, and potato lose ~25% water weight when cooked. Therefore, when determining the raw weight amount based on the cooked weight amount, divide the cooked weight amount by 0.75. On the flip side, oats and quinoa gain weight when cooked due to water retention. Therefore, when determining the uncooked amount based on the cooked amount, divide the cooked amount by 2 for oats, and 3 for quinoa.

Weighing ingredients using a food scale

Utilizing a food scale to measure ingredients is crucial for ensuring the accuracy and precision necessary for your dog's meal preparation. This method guarantees that you're incorporating the exact amount of each component, which is vital for fulfilling your dog's nutritional requirements effectively. Measuring ingredients by weight, in grams or ounces, offers consistent and exact measurements. In contrast, volume measurements like cups, are not as reliable due to variations in how ingredients are compacted. For example, a cup of flour can weigh anywhere from 3.5 to 5.5 ounces depending on how you fill the cup. This inconsistency underscores the advantage of using a food scale, which allows for switching between grams and ounces, ensuring precision. When using a food scale, simply place your mixing bowl on top of it, and zero out the scale before adding each ingredient. This eliminates the need for leveling off measuring cups or switching utensils. Opting to measure by weight streamlines the process, making it quicker, simpler, and cleaner, ensuring your homemade recipes are consistently successful.

Powders, oils and natural supplements

Ingredients such as eggshell powder, kelp powder, hempseed oil, and natural supplements such as vitamin D and E drops should be added only after the food has cooled to room temperature. Why? Heat can degrade these sensitive nutrients, reducing their effectiveness before your dog even gets a chance to benefit from them. Also, mixing them in with the other ingredients after the cooking process is complete ensures even distribution throughout the food.

Storage and thawing

As a reminder, you've got a three-day window to keep those prepped meals in the fridge. Beyond that, the freezer is your best friend, but only up to a month to prevent nutrient loss. Make sure to thaw food in the fridge and not at room temperature or in the microwave. Remember, some foods might get a bit of a texture tweak once frozen, which could be a turn-off for those picky eaters. If your canine companion has a discerning palate, consider smaller batches to keep things fresh and freezer-free. If your pet prefers their food gently warmed, you can use a hot water bath to heat it. Simply place the container of thawed or refrigerated food into a larger bowl or container filled with hot water, allowing the food to warm evenly without cooking it.

By keeping these tips in mind, you will be giving your dog the best nutrition possible. It's all about precision, care, and a little love—because, at the end of the day, our dogs are family, and deserve meals made with just as much thought and attention as our own. So, let's get cooking!

Egg Shell Powder

Cooking Instructions:

1. Preheat your oven to 300°F.

2. Rinse the eggshells thoroughly under cold water.

3. Place the rinsed eggshells in an oven-safe dish.

4. Bake for 5–7 minutes, or until the shells are completely dry.

5. Once cooled, grind the eggshells using a blender, food processor, or coffee grinder until they reach a fine powder consistency.

6. Store the powder in an airtight container in a cool, dry place, or in the freezer, for up to two months.

Chicken, Oyster and Kale

Protein: 57.7%, Fat 26.7%, Carbohydrate: 9.2%, Minerals: 6.4% *(calculated based on dry matter)*

Total Calories: 1498 kcals *(1.3 kcals per gram or 37.3 kcals per ounce of food)*

Total Recipe Amount: 1140g or 40.2oz

This meal is considered High Protein, Moderate Fat, Low Carb.

Ingredients:	Grams:	Ounces:
Chicken breast, skinless, gently cooked	500 g	17.6 oz
Chicken, dark meat, with skin & fat, gently cooked	200 g	7.1 oz
Kale, raw	100 g	3.5 oz
Oysters, raw or canned in water	100 g	3.5 oz
Spinach, boiled, drained, no salt	80 g	2.8 oz
Sweet potato, gently cooked	50 g	1.8 oz
Egg yolk	50 g	1.8 oz
Apples, with skin, raw	30 g	1.1 oz
Hempseed oil	20 g	0.7 oz
Egg shell powder	6 g	0.2 oz
Nutritional yeast	3 g	0.1 oz
Kelp, dried, I = 700 mcg/g	0.6 g	0.02 oz
Vitamin D drops, 100 IU/drop, 1 drop is 0.033g	0.033 g	1 drop

Cooking Instructions:

1. **Cook Chicken:** Place the chicken breast and dark meat into the slow cooker and cook on low for 3 hours until tender.

2. **Add Sweet Potato, Kale, & Oysters:** In the last 45 minutes, add the cooked sweet potato, kale, and oysters (raw or canned) to the slow cooker.

3. **Boil Spinach:** Boil the spinach for 2-3 minutes, drain thoroughly, and set aside.

4. **Cool & Combine:** Once cooking is complete, turn off the slow cooker. Let the mixture cool slightly, then stir in the boiled spinach, egg yolks, diced apples, hempseed oil, egg shell powder, nutritional yeast, and kelp.

5. **Add Vitamin D:** After the mixture has fully cooled to room temperature, add the vitamin D drop.

6. **Stir & Blend:** Mix all the ingredients together thoroughly to ensure even distribution.

7. **Portion & Store:** Portion into daily servings. Store in the fridge for 3 days or freeze for up to 1 month.

Daily Meal Portioning based on Dog's Weight:

Tip: If your dog eats two meals a day, divide the total daily amount of food in half and serve it across both meals.

Dog's Weight		Daily Meal Portion			
		Less Active Dog		Active Dog	
Pounds (lbs)	Kilograms (kgs)	Grams	Ounces	Grams	Ounces
5	2	134 g	4.7 oz	155 g	5.5 oz
10	5	225 g	7.9 oz	260 g	9.2 oz
15	7	305 g	10.7 oz	353 g	12.4 oz
20	9	378 g	13.3 oz	437 g	15.4 oz
25	11	447 g	15.8 oz	517 g	18.2 oz
30	14	512 g	18.1 oz	593 g	20.9 oz
35	16	575 g	20.3 oz	666 g	23.5 oz
40	18	635 g	22.4 oz	736 g	26 oz
45	20	694 g	24.5 oz	804 g	28.4 oz
50	23	751 g	26.5 oz	870 g	30.7 oz
55	25	807 g	28.5 oz	934 g	33 oz
60	27	861 g	30.4 oz	997 g	35.2 oz
65	30	914 g	32.3 oz	1059 g	37.4 oz
70	32	967 g	34.1 oz	1119 g	39.5 oz
75	34	1018 g	35.9 oz	1179 g	41.6 oz
80	36	1069 g	37.7 oz	1237 g	43.6 oz
85	39	1118 g	39.5 oz	1295 g	45.7 oz
90	41	1167 g	41.2 oz	1352 g	47.7 oz
95	43	1216 g	42.9 oz	1408 g	49.7 oz
100	45	1263 g	44.6 oz	1463 g	51.6 oz

Chicken, Mushroom and Pumpkin

Protein: 57.1%, Fat: 30.2%, Carbohydrates: 6.9%, Minerals: 5.8% *(calculated based on dry matter)*

Total Calories: 1313 kcals *(1.4 kcals per gram or 39.5 kcals per ounce of food)*

Total Recipe Amount: 943g or 33.2oz

This meal is considered High Protein, Moderate Fat, Low Carb.

Ingredients:	Grams:	Ounces:
Chicken breast, skinless, gently cooked	400 g	14.1 oz
Chicken, dark meat, with skin & fat, gently cooked	200 g	7.1 oz
Mushrooms, button or portobello, raw	100 g	3.5 oz
Pumpkin, canned, without salt	80 g	2.8 oz
Oysters, raw or canned in water	65 g	2.3 oz
Egg yolk	50 g	1.8 oz
Hempseed oil	20 g	0.7 oz
Apples, with skin, raw	15 g	0.5 oz
Egg shell powder	5 g	0.2 oz
Turmeric, ground	5 g	0.2 oz
Nutritional yeast	2 g	0.07 oz
Kelp, dried, I = 700 mcg/g	0.4 g	0.01 oz
Vitamin D drops, 100 IU/drop, 1 drop is 0.033g	0.033 g	1 drop

Cooking Instructions:

1. **Cook Chicken:** Add the chicken breast and dark meat to the slow cooker. Cook on low for 3 hours until tender.

2. **Add Mushrooms & Oysters:** Chop the mushrooms and add them along with the oysters to the slow cooker in the last 30 minutes of cooking.

3. **Mix Pumpkin & Egg Yolk:** After cooking, stir in the canned pumpkin and egg yolks to help bind the ingredients and add moisture.

4. **Cool & Combine:** Let the mixture cool slightly. Add diced apples, hempseed oil, egg shell powder, turmeric, nutritional yeast, and dried kelp. Mix well to combine evenly.

5. **Add Vitamin D:** Once the mixture is fully cooled to room temperature, add the vitamin D drop.

6. **Stir & Blend:** Mix all the ingredients together thoroughly to ensure even distribution.

7. **Portion & Store:** Portion into daily servings. Store in the fridge for 3 days or freeze for up to 1 month.

Daily Meal Portioning based on Dog's Weight:

Tip: If your dog eats two meals a day, divide the total daily amount of food in half and serve it across both meals.

Dog's Weight		Daily Meal Portion			
		Less Active Dog		Active Dog	
Pounds (lbs)	Kilograms (kgs)	Grams	Ounces	Grams	Ounces
5	2	126 g	4.5 oz	146 g	5.1 oz
10	5	212 g	7.5 oz	245 g	8.7 oz
15	7	287 g	10.1 oz	332 g	11.7 oz
20	9	356 g	12.6 oz	413 g	14.6 oz
25	11	421 g	14.9 oz	488 g	17.2 oz
30	14	483 g	17 oz	559 g	19.7 oz
35	16	542 g	19.1 oz	628 g	22.1 oz
40	18	599 g	21.1 oz	694 g	24.5 oz
45	20	655 g	23.1 oz	758 g	26.7 oz
50	23	708 g	25 oz	820 g	28.9 oz
55	25	761 g	26.8 oz	881 g	31.1 oz
60	27	812 g	28.7 oz	940 g	33.2 oz
65	30	862 g	30.4 oz	999 g	35.2 oz
70	32	912 g	32.2 oz	1056 g	37.2 oz
75	34	960 g	33.9 oz	1112 g	39.2 oz
80	36	1008 g	35.6 oz	1167 g	41.2 oz
85	39	1055 g	37.2 oz	1221 g	43.1 oz
90	41	1101 g	38.9 oz	1275 g	45 oz
95	43	1146 g	40.4 oz	1327 g	46.8 oz
100	45	1191 g	42 oz	1379 g	48.7 oz

Chicken, Egg and Squash

Protein: 45.2%, Fat: 37%, Carbohydrate: 11.6%, Minerals: 6.2% *(calculated based on dry matter)*

Total Calories: 994 kcals *(1.5 kcals per gram or 42.3 kcals per ounce of food)*

Total Recipe Amount: 666g or 23.5oz

This meal is considered High Protein, Moderate Fat, and Low Carb.

Ingredients:	Grams:	Ounces:
Chicken, dark meat, with skin & fat, gently cooked	250 g	8.8 oz
Chicken liver, raw	150 g	5.3 oz
Butternut squash, gently cooked	125 g	4.4 oz
1 large egg, raw	50 g	1.8 oz
Oysters, raw or canned in water	50 g	1.8 oz
Apples, raw, with skin	15 g	0.5 oz
Hempseed oil	15 g	0.5 oz
Turmeric, ground	5 g	0.2 oz
Egg shell powder	5 g	0.2 oz
Kelp, dried, I = 700 mcg/g	0.5 g	0.02 oz
Nutritional yeast	0.3 g	0.01 oz
Vitamin D drops, 100 IU/drop, 1 drop is 0.033g	0.033 g	1 drop

Cooking Instructions:

1. **Cook Chicken & Butternut Squash:** Peel and dice the butternut squash. Add the dark meat chicken and diced squash to the slow cooker. Cook on low for 3 hours until the chicken is tender and the squash is soft.

2. **Add Chicken Liver & Oysters:** In the last 30 minutes of cooking, add the chicken liver and oysters (raw or canned) to the slow cooker.

3. **Cool & Combine:** Once cooking is complete, turn off the slow cooker. Allow the mixture to cool slightly, then stir in the egg, diced apples, hempseed oil, egg shell powder, turmeric, nutritional yeast, and dried kelp.

4. **Add Vitamin D:** When the mixture has cooled to room temperature, add the vitamin D drop.

5. **Stir & Blend:** Thoroughly mix all ingredients together to ensure even distribution.

6. **Portion & Store:** Portion into daily servings. Store in the fridge for 3 days or freeze for up to 1 month.

Daily Meal Portioning based on Dog's Weight:

Tip: If your dog eats two meals a day, divide the total daily amount of food in half and serve it across both meals.

Dog's Weight		Daily Meal Portion			
		Less Active Dog		Active Dog	
Pounds (lbs)	Kilograms (kgs)	Grams	Ounces	Grams	Ounces
5	2	118 g	4.2 oz	136 g	4.8 oz
10	5	198 g	7 oz	229 g	8 oz
15	7	268 g	9.5 oz	310 g	11 oz
20	9	333 g	11.7 oz	385 g	13.6 oz
25	11	393 g	13.9 oz	455 g	16 oz
30	14	451 g	16 oz	522 g	18.4 oz
35	16	506 g	17.9 oz	586 g	20.7 oz
40	18	559 g	19.7 oz	648 g	22.9 oz
45	20	611 g	21.6 oz	708 g	25 oz
50	23	661 g	23.3 oz	766 g	27 oz
55	25	710 g	25.1 oz	822 g	29 oz
60	27	758 g	26.7 oz	878 g	31 oz
65	30	805 g	28.4 oz	932 g	32.9 oz
70	32	851 g	30 oz	986 g	34.8 oz
75	34	896 g	31.6 oz	1038 g	36.6 oz
80	36	941 g	33.2 oz	1089 g	38.4 oz
85	39	985 g	34.7 oz	1140 g	40.2 oz
90	41	1028 g	36.3 oz	1190 g	42 oz
95	43	1070 g	37.8 oz	1239 g	43.7 oz
100	45	1112 g	39.2 oz	1288 g	45.4 oz

Chicken, Oyster and Spinach

Protein: 47.5%, Fat 38.9%, Carbohydrate: 7.8%, Minerals: 5.8% *(calculated based on dry matter)*

Total Calories: 1358 kcals *(1.8 kcals per gram or 50.3 kcals per ounce of food)*

Total Recipe Amount: 766g or 27oz

This meal is considered High Protein, Moderate Fat, Low Carb.

Ingredients:	Grams:	Ounces:
Chicken, dark meat, with skin & fat, gently cooked	300 g	10.6 oz
Chicken liver, raw	200 g	7.1 oz
Oysters, raw or canned in water	110 g	3.9 oz
Egg yolk	50 g	1.8 oz
Spinach, boiled, drained, no salt	30 g	1.1 oz
Blueberries, raw	30 g	1.1 oz
Hempseed oil	20 g	0.7 oz
Nutritional yeast	15.5 g	0.6 oz
Egg shell powder	5 g	0.2 oz
Turmeric, ground	5 g	0.2 oz
Kelp, dried, I = 700 mcg/g	0.3 g	0.01 oz
Vitamin D drops, 100 IU/drop, 1 drop is 0.033g	0.033 g	1 drop

Cooking Instructions:

1. **Cook Chicken:** Place the dark meat chicken with skin and fat into the slow cooker. Cook on low for 3 hours until the chicken is tender.

2. **Add Chicken Liver & Oysters:** In the last 30 minutes, add the chicken liver and oysters (raw or canned) to the slow cooker.

3. **Boil Spinach:** While the chicken and liver cook, boil the spinach for 2-3 minutes, drain thoroughly, and set aside.

4. **Cool & Combine:** Once the cooking is complete, turn off the slow cooker and allow the mixture to cool slightly. Stir in the boiled spinach, egg yolks, blueberries, hempseed oil, nutritional yeast, egg shell powder, turmeric, and dried kelp.

5. **Add Vitamin D:** Once the mixture is fully cooled to room temperature, add the vitamin D drop.

6. **Stir & Blend:** Thoroughly mix all ingredients together to ensure even distribution.

7. **Portion & Store:** Portion into daily servings. Store in the fridge for 3 days or freeze for up to 1 month.

Daily Meal Portioning based on Dog's Weight:

Tip: If your dog eats two meals a day, divide the total daily amount of food in half and serve it across both meals.

Dog's Weight		Daily Meal Portion			
		Less Active Dog		Active Dog	
Pounds (lbs)	Kilograms (kgs)	Grams	Ounces	Grams	Ounces
5	2	99 g	3.5 oz	115 g	4 oz
10	5	166 g	5.9 oz	193 g	6.8 oz
15	7	226 g	8 oz	261 g	9.2 oz
20	9	280 g	9.9 oz	324 g	11.4 oz
25	11	331 g	11.7 oz	383 g	13.5 oz
30	14	379 g	13.4 oz	439 g	15.5 oz
35	16	426 g	15 oz	493 g	17.4 oz
40	18	471 g	16.6 oz	545 g	19.2 oz
45	20	514 g	18.1 oz	596 g	21 oz
50	23	557 g	19.6 oz	644 g	22.7 oz
55	25	598 g	21.1 oz	692 g	24.4 oz
60	27	638 g	22.5 oz	739 g	26.1 oz
65	30	678 g	23.9 oz	785 g	27.7 oz
70	32	716 g	25.3 oz	829 g	29.3 oz
75	34	754 g	26.6 oz	874 g	30.8 oz
80	36	792 g	27.9 oz	917 g	32.3 oz
85	39	829 g	29.2 oz	959 g	33.8 oz
90	41	865 g	30.5 oz	1002 g	35.3 oz
95	43	901 g	31.8 oz	1043 g	36.8 oz
100	45	936 g	33 oz	1084 g	38.2 oz

Turkey, Salmon and Broccoli

Protein: 50.3%, Fat: 36.5%, Carbohydrate: 7.2%, Minerals: 6% *(calculated based on dry matter)*

Total Calories: 1220 kcals *(1.5 kcals per gram or 42.4 kcals per ounce of food)*

Total Recipe Amount: 815g or 28.8oz

This meal is considered High Protein, Moderate Fat, Low Carb.

Ingredients:	Grams:	Ounces:
Turkey, 85% lean, gently cooked	280 g	9.9 oz
Turkey liver, raw	200 g	7.1 oz
Broccoli, gently cooked	150 g	5.3 oz
Salmon, gently cooked	60 g	2.1 oz
Oysters, raw or canned in water	35 g	1.2 oz
Pumpkin, canned, without salt	30 g	1.1 oz
Blueberries, raw	30 g	1.1 oz
Hempseed oil	22 g	0.8 oz
Egg shell powder	5 g	0.2 oz
Cinnamon, ground	2 g	0.07 oz
Nutritional yeast	1 g	0.04 oz
Kelp, dried, I = 700 mcg/g	0.4 g	0.01 oz

Cooking Instructions:

1. **Cook Turkey & Broccoli:** Add the lean turkey and broccoli to the slow cooker. Cook on low for 3 hours until the turkey is tender.

2. **Add Turkey Liver & Salmon:** In the last 30 minutes, add the turkey liver and salmon to the slow cooker.

3. **Add Oysters & Pumpkin:** During the last 15 minutes of cooking, stir in the oysters (raw or canned) and canned 100% pure pumpkin.

4. **Cool & Combine:** Once the cooking is complete, turn off the slow cooker and let the mixture cool slightly. Stir in blueberries, hempseed oil, egg shell powder, cinnamon, nutritional yeast, and dried kelp.

5. **Stir & Blend:** Thoroughly mix all ingredients together to ensure even distribution.

6. **Portion & Store:** Portion into daily servings. Store in the fridge for 3 days or freeze for up to 1 month.

Daily Meal Portioning based on Dog's Weight:

Tip: If your dog eats two meals a day, divide the total daily amount of food in half and serve it across both meals.

Dog's Weight		Daily Meal Portion			
		Less Active Dog		Active Dog	
Pounds (lbs)	Kilograms (kgs)	Grams	Ounces	Grams	Ounces
5	2	117 g	4.1 oz	136 g	4.8 oz
10	5	197 g	7 oz	229 g	8.1 oz
15	7	268 g	9.4 oz	310 g	10.9 oz
20	9	332 g	11.7 oz	384 g	13.6 oz
25	11	393 g	13.8 oz	454 g	16 oz
30	14	450 g	15.9 oz	521 g	18.4 oz
35	16	505 g	17.8 oz	585 g	20.6 oz
40	18	558 g	19.7 oz	647 g	22.8 oz
45	20	610 g	21.5 oz	706 g	25 oz
50	23	660 g	23.3 oz	764 g	27 oz
55	25	709 g	25 oz	821 g	29 oz
60	27	757 g	26.7 oz	876 g	31 oz
65	30	804 g	28.4 oz	931 g	32.8 oz
70	32	850 g	30 oz	984 g	34.7 oz
75	34	895 g	31.6 oz	1036 g	36.5 oz
80	36	939 g	33.1 oz	1087 g	38.4 oz
85	39	983 g	34.7 oz	1138 g	40.1 oz
90	41	1026 g	36.2 oz	1188 g	41.9 oz
95	43	1068 g	37.7 oz	1237 g	43.6 oz
100	45	1110 g	39.2 oz	1285 g	45.3 oz

Turkey, Duck and Brussels Sprouts

Protein: 51.7%, Fat 30.7%, Carbohydrate: 11.5%, Minerals: 6.1% *(calculated based on dry matter)*

Total Calories: 1190 kcals *(1.5 kcals per gram or 41.8 kcals per ounce of food)*

Total Recipe Amount: 807g or 28.5oz

This meal is considered High Protein, Moderate Fat, Low Carb.

Ingredients:	Grams:	Ounces:
Turkey, 85% lean, gently cooked	375 g	13.2 oz
Duck liver, raw	200 g	7.1 oz
Brussels sprouts, raw	100 g	3.5 oz
Pumpkin, canned, without salt	50 g	1.8 oz
Blueberries, raw	30 g	1.1 oz
Oysters, raw or canned in water	22 g	0.8 oz
Egg yolk	20 g	0.7 oz
Egg shell powder	5 g	0.2 oz
Nutritional yeast	2 g	0.07 oz
Kelp, dried, I = 700 mcg/g	1.5 g	0.05 oz
Turmeric, ground	1 g	0.04 oz
Vitamin D drops, 100 IU/drop, 1 drop is 0.033g	0.033 g	1 drop
Vitamin E drops, 30 IU/drop, 1 drop is 0.033g	0.033 g	1 drop

Cooking Instructions:

1. **Cook Turkey & Brussels Sprouts:** Add the lean turkey and brussels sprouts to the slow cooker. Cook on low for 3 hours until the turkey is tender.

2. **Add Duck Liver & Oysters:** In the last 30 minutes, add the duck liver and oysters (raw or canned) to the slow cooker.

3. **Add Pumpkin & Egg Yolk:** During the last 15 minutes, stir in the canned 100% pure pumpkin and egg yolk.

4. **Cool & Combine:** Once the cooking is complete, turn off the slow cooker and allow the mixture to cool slightly. Stir in blueberries, egg shell powder, nutritional yeast, kelp, and ground turmeric.

5. **Add Vitamins:** Once cooled to room temperature, add the drops of vitamin D and vitamin E.

6. **Stir & Blend:** Thoroughly mix all ingredients together to ensure even distribution.

7. **Portion & Store:** Portion into daily servings. Store in the fridge for 3 days or freeze for up to 1 month.

Daily Meal Portioning based on Dog's Weight:

Tip: If your dog eats two meals a day, divide the total daily amount of food in half and serve it across both meals.

Dog's Weight		Daily Meal Portion			
		Less Active Dog		Active Dog	
Pounds (lbs)	Kilograms (kgs)	Grams	Ounces	Grams	Ounces
5	2	119 g	4.2 oz	138 g	4.9 oz
10	5	200 g	7.1 oz	232 g	8.2 oz
15	7	271 g	9.6 oz	315 g	11.1 oz
20	9	337 g	11.9 oz	390 g	13.8 oz
25	11	398 g	14 oz	461 g	16.3 oz
30	14	456 g	16.1 oz	528 g	18.6 oz
35	16	512 g	18.1 oz	593 g	20.9 oz
40	18	566 g	20 oz	656 g	23.1 oz
45	20	619 g	21.8 oz	717 g	25.3 oz
50	23	670 g	23.6 oz	775 g	27.3 oz
55	25	719 g	25.4 oz	833 g	29.4 oz
60	27	767 g	27.1 oz	889 g	31.3 oz
65	30	815 g	28.8 oz	944 g	33.3 oz
70	32	862 g	30.4 oz	998 g	35.2 oz
75	34	907 g	32 oz	1051 g	37.1 oz
80	36	952 g	33.6 oz	1103 g	38.9 oz
85	39	997 g	35.2 oz	1154 g	40.7 oz
90	41	1040 g	36.7 oz	1204 g	42.5 oz
95	43	1083 g	38.2 oz	1254 g	44.2 oz
100	45	1126 g	39.7 oz	1303 g	46 oz

Turkey, Oyster and Green Beans

Protein: 48.5%, Fat: 36.8%, Carbohydrate: 8.5%, Minerals: 6.2% *(calculated based on dry matter)*

Total Calories: 1465 kcals *(1.5 kcals per gram or 43 kcals per ounce of food)*

Total Recipe Amount: 966g or 34.1oz

This meal is considered High Protein, Moderate Fat, Low Carb.

Ingredients:	Grams:	Ounces:
Turkey, 85% lean, gently cooked	350 g	12.4 oz
Turkey liver, raw	210 g	7.4 oz
Oysters, raw or canned in water	100 g	3.5 oz
Green beans, raw	100 g	3.5 oz
Mushrooms, button or portobello, raw	60 g	2.1 oz
Butternut squash, gently cooked	60 g	2.1 oz
Sardines, canned in water, no salt	50 g	1.8 oz
Hempseed oil	25 g	0.9 oz
Egg shell powder	5 g	0.2 oz
Kelp, dried, I = 700 mcg/g	5 g	0.2 oz
Nutritional yeast	1 g	0.04 oz

Cooking Instructions:

1. **Cook Turkey & Butternut Squash:** Peel and dice the butternut squash. Add the lean turkey and butternut squash to the slow cooker. Cook on low for 3 hours until the turkey is tender.

2. **Add Turkey Liver & Oysters:** In the last 30 minutes, add the turkey liver and oysters (raw or canned) to the slow cooker.

3. **Add Green Beans & Mushrooms:** During the last 15 minutes, stir in the green beans and mushrooms (button or portobello).

4. **Cool & Combine:** Once the cooking is complete, turn off the slow cooker and allow the mixture to cool slightly. Stir in the canned sardines, hempseed oil, egg shell powder, nutritional yeast, and dried kelp.

5. **Stir & Blend:** Thoroughly mix all ingredients together to ensure even distribution.

6. **Portion & Store:** Portion into daily servings. Store in the fridge for 3 days or freeze for up to 1 month.

Daily Meal Portioning based on Dog's Weight:

Tip: If your dog eats two meals a day, divide the total daily amount of food in half and serve it across both meals.

Dog's Weight		Daily Meal Portion			
		Less Active Dog		Active Dog	
Pounds (lbs)	Kilograms (kgs)	Grams	Ounces	Grams	Ounces
5	2	116 g	4.1 oz	134 g	4.7 oz
10	5	195 g	6.9 oz	225 g	8 oz
15	7	264 g	9.3 oz	306 g	10.8 oz
20	9	327 g	11.6 oz	379 g	13.4 oz
25	11	387 g	13.7 oz	448 g	15.8 oz
30	14	444 g	15.7 oz	514 g	18.1 oz
35	16	498 g	17.6 oz	577 g	20.3 oz
40	18	551 g	19.4 oz	637 g	22.5 oz
45	20	601 g	21.2 oz	696 g	24.6 oz
50	23	651 g	23 oz	754 g	26.6 oz
55	25	699 g	24.7 oz	809 g	28.6 oz
60	27	746 g	26.3 oz	864 g	30.5 oz
65	30	792 g	28 oz	918 g	32.4 oz
70	32	838 g	29.6 oz	967 g	34.2 oz
75	34	882 g	31.1 oz	1021 g	36 oz
80	36	926 g	32.7 oz	1072 g	37.8 oz
85	39	969 g	34.2 oz	1122 g	39.6 oz
90	41	1011 g	35.7 oz	1171 g	41.3 oz
95	43	1053 g	37.2 oz	1220 g	43 oz
100	45	1095 g	38.6 oz	1267 g	44.7 oz

Turkey, Salmon and Oyster

Protein: 50.7%, Fat 34.9%, Carbohydrate: 7.9%, Minerals: 6.5% *(calculated based on dry matter)*

Total Calories: 1017 kcals *(1.8 kcals per gram or 51.4 kcals per ounce of food)*

Total Recipe Amount: 561g or 19.8oz

This meal is considered High Protein, Moderate Fat, Low Carb.

Ingredients:	Grams:	Ounces:
Turkey, 85% lean, gently cooked	200 g	7.1 oz
Turkey liver, raw	150 g	5.3 oz
Salmon, gently cooked	85 g	3 oz
Oysters, raw or canned in water	50 g	1.8 oz
Quinoa, cooked	40 g	1.4 oz
Hempseed oil	18 g	0.6 oz
Turmeric, ground	6 g	0.2 oz
Egg shell powder	5 g	0.2 oz
Nutritional yeast	5 g	0.2 oz
Kelp, dried, I = 700 mcg/g	2 g	0.07 oz

Cooking Instructions:

1. **Cook Turkey & Quinoa:** Add the lean turkey and cooked quinoa to the slow cooker. Cook on low for 2-3 hours until the turkey is tender.

2. **Add Turkey Liver & Salmon:** In the last 30 minutes, add the turkey liver and salmon to the slow cooker.

3. **Add Oysters:** During the last 15 minutes, stir in the oysters (raw or canned in water).

4. **Cool & Combine:** Once cooking is complete, turn off the slow cooker and allow the mixture to cool slightly. Stir in hempseed oil, turmeric, egg shell powder, nutritional yeast, and dried kelp.

5. **Stir & Blend:** Thoroughly mix all ingredients together to ensure even distribution.

6. **Portion & Store:** Portion into daily servings. Store in the fridge for 3 days or freeze for up to 1 month.

Daily Meal Portioning based on Dog's Weight:

Tip: If your dog eats two meals a day, divide the total daily amount of food in half and serve it across both meals.

Dog's Weight		Daily Meal Portion			
		Less Active Dog		Active Dog	
Pounds (lbs)	Kilograms (kgs)	Grams	Ounces	Grams	Ounces
5	2	97 g	3.4 oz	112 g	4 oz
10	5	163 g	5.7 oz	189 g	6.7 oz
15	7	221 g	7.8 oz	256 g	9 oz
20	9	274 g	9.7 oz	317 g	11.2 oz
25	11	324 g	11.4 oz	375 g	13.2 oz
30	14	371 g	13.1 oz	430 g	15.2 oz
35	16	417 g	14.7 oz	482 g	17 oz
40	18	461 g	16.3 oz	533 g	18.9 oz
45	20	503 g	17.8 oz	583 g	20.6 oz
50	23	545 g	19.2 oz	630 g	22.2 oz
55	25	585 g	20.6 oz	677 g	23.9 oz
60	27	624 g	22 oz	723 g	25.5 oz
65	30	663 g	23.4 oz	768 g	27.1 oz
70	32	701 g	24.7 oz	811 g	28.6 oz
75	34	738 g	26 oz	855 g	30.1 oz
80	36	775 g	27.3 oz	897 g	31.6 oz
85	39	811 g	28.6 oz	939 g	33.1 oz
90	41	846 g	30 oz	980 g	34.6 oz
95	43	881 g	31.1 oz	1020 g	36 oz
100	45	916 g	32.3 oz	1060 g	37.4 oz

Turkey, Duck and Broccoli

Protein: 41.2%, Fat: 34.5%, Carbohydrate: 18.7%, Minerals: 5.6% *(calculated based on dry matter)*

Total Calories: 1331 kcals *(1.9 kcals per gram or 53.3 kcals per ounce of food)*

Total Recipe Amount: 709g or 25oz

This meal is considered High Protein, Moderate Fat, Moderate Carb.

Ingredients:	Grams:	Ounces:
Turkey, 85% lean, gently cooked	300 g	10.6 oz
Broccoli, gently cooked	80 g	2.8 oz
Duck liver, raw	60 g	2.1 oz
Brown rice, cooked	60 g	2.1 oz
Blueberries, raw	50 g	1.8 oz
Egg yolk	50 g	1.8 oz
Oysters, raw or canned in water	40 g	1.4 oz
Nutritional yeast	37 g	1.3 oz
Hempseed oil	22 g	0.8 oz
Egg shell powder	5 g	0.2 oz
Kelp, dried, I = 700 mcg/g	4.5 g	0. 16 oz
Vitamin D drops, 100 IU/drop, 1 drop is 0.033g	0.033 g	1 drop

Cooking Instructions:

1. **Cook Turkey & Broccoli:** Add the lean turkey and broccoli to the slow cooker. Cook on low for 3 hours until the turkey is tender.

2. **Add Duck Liver & Oysters:** In the last 30 minutes, add the duck liver and oysters (raw or canned) to the slow cooker.

3. **Cool & Combine:** Once the cooking is complete, turn off the slow cooker and allow the mixture to cool slightly. Stir in the pre-cooked brown rice, blueberries, egg yolk, hempseed oil, nutritional yeast, egg shell powder, and dried kelp.

4. **Add Vitamin D:** Once the mixture has cooled to room temperature, add the vitamin D drop.

5. **Stir & Blend:** Thoroughly mix all ingredients together to ensure even distribution.

6. **Portion & Store:** Portion into daily servings. Store in the fridge for 3 days or freeze for up to 1 month.

Daily Meal Portioning based on Dog's Weight:

Tip: If your dog eats two meals a day, divide the total daily amount of food in half and serve it across both meals.

Dog's Weight		Daily Meal Portion			
		Less Active Dog		Active Dog	
Pounds (lbs)	Kilograms (kgs)	Grams	Ounces	Grams	Ounces
5	2	94 g	3.3 oz	108 g	3.8 oz
10	5	157 g	5.5 oz	182 g	6.4 oz
15	7	213 g	7.5 oz	247 g	8.7 oz
20	9	264 g	9.3 oz	306 g	10.8 oz
25	11	313 g	11 oz	362 g	12.8 oz
30	14	358 g	12.6 oz	415 g	14.6 oz
35	16	402 g	14.2 oz	466 g	16.4 oz
40	18	445 g	15.7 oz	515 g	18.2 oz
45	20	486 g	17.1 oz	562 g	19.8 oz
50	23	526 g	18.5 oz	609 g	21.5 oz
55	25	565 g	19.9 oz	654 g	23.1 oz
60	27	603 g	21.3 oz	698 g	24.6 oz
65	30	640 g	22.6 oz	741 g	26 oz
70	32	676 g	23.9 oz	783 g	27.6 oz
75	34	712 g	25 oz	825 g	29.1 oz
80	36	748 g	26.4 oz	866 g	30.5 oz
85	39	782 g	27.6 oz	906 g	32 oz
90	41	817 g	28.8 oz	946 g	33.4 oz
95	43	851 g	30 oz	985 g	34.7 oz
100	45	884 g	31.2 oz	1023 g	36.1 oz

Turkey, Oyster and Kale

Protein: 51.6%, Fat: 28.5%, Carbohydrate: 13.2%, Minerals: 6.7% (calculated based on dry matter)

Total Calories: 1228 kcals (1.2 kcals per gram or 35.1 kcals per ounce of food)

Total Recipe Amount: 991g or 35oz

This meal is considered High Protein, Moderate Fat, Low Carb.

Ingredients:	Grams:	Ounces:
Turkey, 85% lean, gently cooked	350 g	12.4 oz
Turkey liver, raw	250 g	8.8 oz
Kale, raw	175 g	6.2 oz
Oysters, raw	80 g	2.8 oz
Mushrooms, button or portobello, raw	50 g	1.8 oz
Sweet potato, gently cooked	50 g	1.8 oz
Blueberries, raw	30 g	1.1 oz
Egg shell powder	5 g	0.2 oz
Kelp, dried, I = 700 mcg/g	0.5 g	0.02 oz
Nutritional yeast	0.3 g	0.01 oz
Vitamin E drops, 30 IU/drop, 1 drop is 0.033g	0.033 g	1 drop

Cooking Instructions:

1. **Cook Turkey & Sweet Potato:** Add the lean turkey and diced sweet potato to the slow cooker. Cook on low for 3 hours until the turkey is tender.

2. **Add Turkey Liver & Oysters:** In the last 30 minutes, add the turkey liver and oysters to the slow cooker.

3. **Add Kale & Mushrooms:** In the last 15 minutes, stir in the kale and mushrooms (button or portobello).

4. **Cool & Combine:** Once cooking is complete, turn off the slow cooker and allow the mixture to cool slightly. Stir in blueberries, egg shell powder, nutritional yeast, and dried kelp.

5. **Add Vitamin E:** Once the mixture has cooled to room temperature, add the vitamin E drop.

6. **Stir & Blend:** Thoroughly mix all ingredients together to ensure even distribution.

7. **Portion & Store:** Portion into daily servings. Store in the fridge for 3 days or freeze for up to 1 month.

Daily Meal Portioning based on Dog's Weight:

Tip: If your dog eats two meals a day, divide the total daily amount of food in half and serve it across both meals.

Dog's Weight		Daily Meal Portion			
		Less Active Dog		Active Dog	
Pounds (lbs)	Kilograms (kgs)	Grams	Ounces	Grams	Ounces
5	2	142 g	5 oz	164 g	5.8 oz
10	5	238 g	8.4 oz	276 g	9.7 oz
15	7	323 g	11.4 oz	374 g	13.2 oz
20	9	401 g	14.1 oz	464 g	16.4 oz
25	11	474 g	16.7 oz	549 g	19.4 oz
30	14	543 g	19.2 oz	629 g	22.2 oz
35	16	610 g	21.5 oz	706 g	24.9 oz
40	18	674 g	23.8 oz	781 g	27.5 oz
45	20	736 g	26 oz	853 g	30.1 oz
50	23	797 g	28.1 oz	923 g	32.6 oz
55	25	856 g	30.2 oz	991 g	35 oz
60	27	914 g	32.2 oz	1058 g	37.3 oz
65	30	970 g	34.2 oz	1123 g	39.6 oz
70	32	1026 g	36.2 oz	1188 g	41.9 oz
75	34	1080 g	38.1 oz	1251 g	44.1 oz
80	36	1134 g	40 oz	1313 g	46.3 oz
85	39	1186 g	41.9 oz	1374 g	48.5 oz
90	41	1239 g	43.7 oz	1434 g	50.6 oz
95	43	1290 g	45.5 oz	1493 g	52.7 oz
100	45	1340 g	47.3 oz	1552 g	54.7 oz

Beef, Salmon and Kale

Protein: 50.5%, Fat: 31.1%, Carb: 12.3%, Minerals: 6.1% *(calculated based on dry matter)*

Total Calories: 1323 kcals *(1.5 kcals per gram or 41.9 kcals per ounce of food)*

Total Recipe Amount: 895g or 31.6oz

This meal is considered High Protein, Moderate Fat, Low Carb.

Ingredients:	Grams:	Ounces:
Ground beef, 85% lean, gently cooked	300 g	10.6 oz
Beef liver, gently cooked	200 g	7.1 oz
Kale, raw	200 g	7.1 oz
Salmon, gently cooked	80 g	2.8 oz
Oysters, raw or canned in water	50 g	1.8 oz
Mangoes, raw, diced, fresh or frozen	40 g	1.4 oz
Hempseed oil	18 g	0.6 oz
Egg shell powder	5 g	0.2 oz
Nutritional yeast	1.5 g	0.05 oz
Kelp, dried, I = 700 mcg/g	0.6 g	0.02 oz

Cooking Instructions:

1. **Cook Ground Beef & Kale:** Add the ground beef and kale to the slow cooker. Cook on low for 2-3 hours until the beef is tender and the kale has wilted.

2. **Add Beef Liver & Salmon:** In the last 30 minutes, add the beef liver and salmon to the slow cooker.

3. **Add Oysters & Mangoes:** During the last 15 minutes of cooking, stir in the oysters and diced mangoes (fresh or frozen).

4. **Cool & Combine:** Once the cooking is complete, turn off the slow cooker and allow the mixture to cool slightly. Stir in hempseed oil, egg shell powder, nutritional yeast, and dried kelp.

5. **Stir & Blend:** Thoroughly mix all ingredients together to ensure even distribution.

6. **Portion & Store:** Portion into daily servings. Store in the fridge for 3 days or freeze for up to 1 month.

Daily Meal Portioning based on Dog's Weight:

Tip: If your dog eats two meals a day, divide the total daily amount of food in half and serve it across both meals.

Dog's Weight		Daily Meal Portion			
		Less Active Dog		Active Dog	
Pounds (lbs)	Kilograms (kgs)	Grams	Ounces	Grams	Ounces
5	2	119 g	4.2 oz	138 g	4.9 oz
10	5	200 g	7.1 oz	231 g	8.2 oz
15	7	271 g	9.6 oz	314 g	11.1 oz
20	9	336 g	11.9 oz	389 g	13.7 oz
25	11	397 g	14 oz	460 g	16.2 oz
30	14	455 g	16.1 oz	527 g	18.6 oz
35	16	511 g	18 oz	592 g	20.9 oz
40	18	565 g	20 oz	654 g	23.1 oz
45	20	618 g	21.8 oz	715 g	25.2 oz
50	23	668 g	23.6 oz	773 g	27.3 oz
55	25	717 g	25.3 oz	831 g	29.3 oz
60	27	766 g	27 oz	887 g	31.3 oz
65	30	813 g	28.7 oz	942 g	33.2 oz
70	32	860 g	30.3 oz	995 g	35.1 oz
75	34	905 g	32 oz	1048 g	37 oz
80	36	950 g	33.5 oz	1100 g	38.8 oz
85	39	994 g	35.1 oz	1151 g	40.6 oz
90	41	1038 g	36.6 oz	1202 g	42.4 oz
95	43	1081 g	38.1 oz	1252 g	44.1 oz
100	45	1123 g	39.6 oz	1301 g	45.9 oz

Beef, Oyster and Vegetables

Protein: 50%, Fat: 36.6%, Carbohydrate: 7.7%, Minerals: 5.7% *(calculated based on dry matter)*

Total Calories: 1396 kcals *(1.6 kcals per gram or 45.9 kcals per ounce of food)*

Total Recipe Amount: 861g or 30.4oz

This meal is considered High Protein, Moderate Fat, Low Carb.

Ingredients:	Grams:	Ounces:
Ground beef, 85% lean, gently cooked	380 g	13.4 oz
Beef liver, gently cooked	200 g	7.1 oz
Oysters, raw or canned in water	100 g	3.5 oz
Spinach, boiled, drained, no salt	50 g	1.8 oz
Zucchini, includes skin, gently cooked	50 g	1.8 oz
Green beans, raw	50 g	1.8 oz
Hempseed oil	24 g	0.9 oz
Egg shell powder	5 g	0.2 oz
Nutritional yeast	1.5 g	0.05 oz
Kelp, dried, I = 700 mcg/g	0.4 g	0.01 oz
Vitamin D drops, 100 IU/drop, 1 drop is 0.033g	0.033 g	1 drop

Cooking Instructions:

1. **Cook Ground Beef & Zucchini:** Add the ground beef and diced zucchini to the slow cooker. Cook on low for 2-3 hours until the beef is tender.

2. **Add Beef Liver & Oysters:** In the last 30 minutes, add the beef liver and oysters to the slow cooker.

3. **Add Spinach & Green Beans:** During the last 15 minutes of cooking, stir in the boiled spinach (drained, no salt) and green beans.

4. **Cool & Combine:** Once the cooking is complete, turn off the slow cooker and allow the mixture to cool slightly. Stir in hempseed oil, egg shell powder, nutritional yeast, and dried kelp.

5. **Add Vitamin D:** Once the mixture is fully cooled to room temperature, add the vitamin D drop.

6. **Stir & Blend:** Thoroughly mix all ingredients together to ensure even distribution.

7. **Portion & Store:** Portion into daily servings. Store in the fridge for 3 days or freeze for up to 1 month.

Daily Meal Portioning based on Dog's Weight:

Tip: If your dog eats two meals a day, divide the total daily amount of food in half and serve it across both meals.

Dog's Weight		Daily Meal Portion			
		Less Active Dog		Active Dog	
Pounds (lbs)	Kilograms (kgs)	Grams	Ounces	Grams	Ounces
5	2	108 g	3.8 oz	125 g	4.4 oz
10	5	182 g	6.4 oz	211 g	7.5 oz
15	7	247 g	8.7 oz	286 g	10.1 oz
20	9	306 g	10.8 oz	355 g	12.5 oz
25	11	362 g	12.8 oz	419 g	14.8 oz
30	14	415 g	14.6 oz	481 g	17 oz
35	16	466 g	16.5 oz	540 g	19 oz
40	18	515 g	18.2 oz	597 g	21 oz
45	20	563 g	19.9 oz	652 g	23 oz
50	23	609 g	21.5 oz	705 g	24.9 oz
55	25	654 g	23.1 oz	758 g	26.7 oz
60	27	699 g	24.6 oz	809 g	28.5 oz
65	30	742 g	26.2 oz	859 g	30.3 oz
70	32	784 g	27.7 oz	908 g	32 oz
75	34	826 g	29.1 oz	956 g	33.7 oz
80	36	867 g	30.6 oz	1004 g	35.4 oz
85	39	907 g	32 oz	1050 g	37 oz
90	41	947 g	33.4 oz	1096 g	38.6 oz
95	43	986 g	34.8 oz	1142 g	40.3 oz
100	45	1025 g	36.1 oz	1186 g	41.9 oz

Beef, Sweet Potato and Vegetables

Protein: 50%, Fat: 30.8%, Carbohydrate: 13.4%, Minerals: 5.8% *(calculated based on dry matter)*

Total Calories: 1040 kcals *(1.6 kcals per gram or 46.5 kcals per ounce of food)*

Total Recipe Amount: 634g or 22.4oz

This meal is considered High Protein, Moderate Fat, Low Carb.

Ingredients:	Grams:	Ounces:
Ground beef, 85% lean, gently cooked	300 g	10.6 oz
Beef liver, gently cooked	200 g	7.1 oz
Sweet potato, gently cooked	50 g	1.8 oz
Green bell peppers, raw, chopped	30 g	1.1 oz
Carrots, raw, grated	30 g	1.1 oz
Flaxseeds	10 g	0.4 oz
Egg shell powder	5 g	0.2 oz
Hempseed oil	5 g	0.2 oz
Turmeric, ground	2 g	0.07 oz
Nutritional yeast	1 g	0.04 oz
Kelp, dried, I = 700 mcg/g	0.5 g	0.02 oz
Vitamin D drops, 100 IU/drop, 1 drop is 0.033g	0.033 g	1 drop
Vitamin E drops, 30 IU/drop, 1 drop is 0.033g	0.033 g	1 drop

Cooking Instructions:

1. **Cook Ground Beef & Sweet Potato:** Add the ground beef and diced sweet potato to the slow cooker. Cook on low for 3 hours until the beef is fully cooked and the sweet potato is tender.

2. **Add Beef Liver:** In the last 30 minutes, add the beef liver to the slow cooker.

3. **Add Vegetables:** During the last 15 minutes of cooking, stir in the chopped green bell peppers and grated carrots.

4. **Cool & Combine:** Once the cooking is complete, turn off the slow cooker and allow the mixture to cool slightly. Stir in flaxseeds, hempseed oil, egg shell powder, ground turmeric, nutritional yeast, and dried kelp.

5. **Add Vitamins:** Once the mixture has cooled to room temperature, add the drops of vitamin D and vitamin E.

6. **Stir & Blend:** Thoroughly mix all ingredients together to ensure even distribution.

7. **Portion & Store:** Portion into daily servings. Store in the fridge for 3 days or freeze for up to 1 month.

Daily Meal Portioning based on Dog's Weight:

Tip: If your dog eats two meals a day, divide the total daily amount of food in half and serve it across both meals.

Dog's Weight		Daily Meal Portion			
		Less Active Dog		Active Dog	
Pounds (lbs)	Kilograms (kgs)	Grams	Ounces	Grams	Ounces
5	2	107 g	3.8 oz	124 g	4.4 oz
10	5	179.9 g	6.3 oz	208 g	7.4 oz
15	7	244 g	8.6 oz	282 g	350 oz
20	9	302 g	10.7 oz	350 g	12.4 oz
25	11	358 g	12.6 oz	414 g	14.6 oz
30	14	410 g	14.5 oz	475 g	16.7 oz
35	16	460 g	16.2 oz	533 g	18.8 oz
40	18	509 g	18 oz	589 g	20.8 oz
45	20	556 g	19.6 oz	643 g	22.7 oz
50	23	601 g	21.2 oz	696 g	24.6 oz
55	25	646 g	22.8 oz	748 g	26.4 oz
60	27	689 g	24.3 oz	798 g	28.2 oz
65	30	732 g	25.8 oz	848 g	29.9 oz
70	32	774 g	27.3 oz	896 g	31.6 oz
75	34	815 g	28.8 oz	944 g	33.3 oz
80	36	855 g	30.2 oz	991 g	35 oz
85	39	895 g	31.6 oz	1037 g	36.6 oz
90	41	935 g	33 oz	1082 g	38.2 oz
95	43	973 g	34.3 oz	1127 g	39.8 oz
100	45	1011 g	35.7 oz	1171 g	41.3 oz

Beef, Cod and Mussels

Protein: 65%, Fat: 13.2%, Carbohydrate: 12.3%, Minerals: 9.5% *(calculated based on dry matter)*

Total Calories: 476 kcals (1.1 kcals per gram or 30 kcals per ounce of food)

Total Recipe Amount: 450g or 15.9oz

This meal is considered High Protein, Low Fat, Low Carb.

Ingredients:	Grams:	Ounces:
Beef liver, gently cooked	200 g	7.1 oz
Atlantic cod, gently cooked	100 g	2.5 oz
Mussels, raw or canned	80 g	2.8 oz
Green bell peppers, raw, chopped	30 g	1.1 oz
Pumpkin, canned, without salt	30 g	1.1 oz
Egg shell powder	5 g	0.2 oz
Hempseed oil	5 g	0.2 oz
Vitamin E drops, 30 IU/drop, 1 drop is 0.033g	0.033 g	1 drop

Cooking Instructions:

1. **Cook Beef Liver & Cod:** Add the beef liver and Atlantic cod to the slow cooker. Cook on low for 3 hours until both are fully cooked.

2. **Add Mussels:** In the last 30 minutes, add the raw or canned mussels to the slow cooker.

3. **Add Vegetables & Pumpkin:** During the last 15 minutes of cooking, stir in the chopped green bell peppers and canned 100% pure pumpkin.

4. **Cool & Combine:** Once cooking is complete, turn off the slow cooker and allow the mixture to cool slightly. Stir in hempseed oil and egg shell powder.

5. **Add Vitamin E:** Once the mixture has cooled to room temperature, add the vitamin E drop.

6. **Stir & Blend:** Thoroughly mix all ingredients together to ensure even distribution.

7. **Portion & Store:** Portion into daily servings. Store in the fridge for 3 days or freeze for up to 1 month.

Daily Meal Portioning based on Dog's Weight:

Tip: If your dog eats two meals a day, divide the total daily amount of food in half and serve it across both meals.

Dog's Weight		Daily Meal Portion			
		Less Active Dog		Active Dog	
Pounds (lbs)	Kilograms (kgs)	Grams	Ounces	Grams	Ounces
5	2	166 g	5.9 oz	192 g	6.8 oz
10	5	279 g	9.8 oz	323 g	11.4 oz
15	7	378 g	13.4 oz	438 g	15.5 oz
20	9	470 g	16.6 oz	544 g	19.2 oz
25	11	555 g	19.6 oz	643 g	22.7 oz
30	14	636 g	22.5 oz	737 g	26 oz
35	16	714 g	25.2 oz	827 g	29.2 oz
40	18	790 g	27.9 oz	914 g	32.3 oz
45	20	863 g	30.4 oz	999 g	35.2 oz
50	23	934 g	32.9 oz	1081 g	38.1 oz
55	25	1003 g	35.4 oz	1161 g	41 oz
60	27	1070 g	37.8 oz	1239 g	43.7 oz
65	30	1137 g	40.1 oz	1316 g	46.4 oz
70	32	1202 g	42.4 oz	1391 g	49 oz
75	34	1265 g	44.6 oz	1465 g	51.7 oz
80	36	1328 g	46.9 oz	1538 g	54.2 oz
85	39	1390 g	49 oz	1609 g	56.8 oz
90	41	1451 g	51.2 oz	1680 g	59.3 oz
95	43	1511 g	53.3 oz	1749 g	61.7 oz
100	45	1570 g	55.4 oz	1818 g	64.1 oz

Beef, Egg and Squash

Protein: 51.1%, Fat: 29.2%, Carbohydrate: 13.1%, Minerals: 6.6% *(calculated based on dry matter)*

Total Calories: 876 kcals *(1.5 kcals per gram or 42.7 kcals per ounce of food)*

Total Recipe Amount: 581g or 20.5oz

This meal is considered High Protein, Moderate Fat, and Low Carb.

Ingredients:	Grams:	Ounces:
Ground beef, 85% lean, gently cooked	250 g	8.8 oz
Beef liver, gently cooked	160 g	5.6 oz
1 large egg, raw	50 g	1.8 oz
Butternut squash, gently cooked	50 g	1.8 oz
Zucchini, includes skin, gently cooked	50 g	1.8 oz
Turmeric, ground	12 g	0.4 oz
Egg shell powder	5 g	0.2 oz
Hempseed oil	2 g	0.07 oz
Nutritional yeast	0.7 g	0.02 oz
Kelp, dried, I = 700 mcg/g	0.3 g	0.01 oz
Vitamin D drops, 100 IU/drop, 1 drop is 0.033g	0.033 g	1 drop
Vitamin E drops, 30 IU/drop, 1 drop is 0.033g	0.033 g	1 drop

Cooking Instructions:

1. **Cook Ground Beef & Vegetables:** Add the ground beef, diced butternut squash, and diced zucchini (with skin) to the slow cooker. Cook on low for 3 hours until the beef is fully cooked and the vegetables are tender.

2. **Add Beef Liver:** In the last 30 minutes, add the beef liver to the slow cooker and cook until done.

3. **Add Raw Egg:** In the last 15 minutes, crack the raw egg into the slow cooker and stir gently to combine.

4. **Cool & Combine:** Once cooking is complete, turn off the slow cooker and allow the mixture to cool slightly. Stir in hempseed oil, egg shell powder, ground turmeric, nutritional yeast, and dried kelp.

5. **Add Vitamins:** Once the mixture has cooled to room temperature, add the drops of vitamin D and vitamin E.

6. **Stir & Blend:** Thoroughly mix all ingredients together to ensure even distribution.

7. **Portion & Store:** Portion into daily servings. Store in the fridge for 3 days or freeze for up to 1 month.

Daily Meal Portioning based on Dog's Weight:

Tip: If your dog eats two meals a day, divide the total daily amount of food in half and serve it across both meals.

Dog's Weight		Daily Meal Portion			
		Less Active Dog		Active Dog	
Pounds (lbs)	Kilograms (kgs)	Grams	Ounces	Grams	Ounces
5	2	117 g	4.1 oz	135 g	4.8 oz
10	5	196 g	7 oz	227 g	8 oz
15	7	266 g	9.4 oz	307 g	10.9 oz
20	9	330 g	11.6 oz	382 g	13.5 oz
25	11	390 g	13.7 oz	451 g	15.9 oz
30	14	447 g	15.8 oz	517 g	18.2 oz
35	16	501 g	17.7 oz	581 g	20.5 oz
40	18	554 g	19.6 oz	642 g	22.6 oz
45	20	605 g	21.4 oz	701 g	24.7 oz
50	23	655 g	23.1 oz	759 g	26.8 oz
55	25	704 g	24.8 oz	815 g	28.7 oz
60	27	751 g	26.5 oz	870 g	30.7 oz
65	30	798 g	28.1 oz	924 g	32.6 oz
70	32	843 g	29.7 oz	976 g	34.4 oz
75	34	888 g	31.3 oz	1028 g	36.3 oz
80	36	932 g	32.9 oz	1079 g	38.1 oz
85	39	875 g	34.4 oz	1129 g	39.8 oz
90	41	1018 g	35.9 oz	1179 g	41.6 oz
95	43	1060 g	37.4 oz	1228 g	43.3 oz
100	45	1102 g	38.9 oz	1276 g	45 oz

Beef, Oyster and Salmon

Protein: 50.4%, Fat: 36.4%, Carbohydrate: 7.2%, Minerals: 6% *(calculated based on dry matter)*

Total Calories: 1309 kcals *(1.7 kcals per gram or 47.6 kcals per ounce of food)*

Total Recipe Amount: 780g or 27.5oz

This meal is High Protein, Moderate Fat, Low Carb.

Ingredients:	Grams:	Ounces:
Ground beef, 85% lean, gently cooked	340 g	12 oz
Beef liver, gently cooked	100 g	3.5 oz
Oysters, raw or canned in water	100 g	3.5 oz
Salmon, gently cooked	60 g	2.1 oz
Spinach, boiled, drained, no salt	50 g	1.8 oz
Duck liver, raw	40 g	1.4 oz
Green bell peppers, raw, chopped	30 g	1.1 oz
Blueberries, raw	30 g	1.1 oz
Hempseed oil	22 g	0.8 oz
Egg shell powder	5 g	0.2 oz
Kelp, dried, I = 700 mcg/g	2 g	0.07 oz
Nutritional yeast	0.9 g	0.03 oz

Cooking Instructions:

1. **Cook Ground Beef & Salmon:** Add the ground beef and salmon to the slow cooker. Cook on low for 3 hours until the beef and salmon are fully cooked.

2. **Add Beef Liver & Duck Liver:** In the last 30 minutes, add the beef liver and duck liver to the slow cooker.

3. **Add Oysters & Spinach:** In the last 15 minutes, add the oysters (raw or canned in water) and the boiled, drained spinach.

4. **Cool & Combine:** Once cooking is complete, turn off the slow cooker and allow the mixture to cool slightly. Stir in the chopped green bell peppers, blueberries, hempseed oil, egg shell powder, nutritional yeast, and dried kelp.

5. **Stir & Blend:** Thoroughly mix all ingredients together to ensure even distribution.

6. **Portion & Store:** Portion into daily servings. Store in the fridge for 3 days or freeze for up to 1 month.

Daily Meal Portioning based on Dog's Weight:

Tip: If your dog eats two meals a day, divide the total daily amount of food in half and serve it across both meals.

Dog's Weight		Daily Meal Portion			
		Less Active Dog		Active Dog	
Pounds (lbs)	Kilograms (kgs)	Grams	Ounces	Grams	Ounces
5	2	105 g	3.7 oz	121 g	4.3 oz
10	5	176 g	6.2 oz	204 g	7.2 oz
15	7	239 g	8.4 oz	276 g	9.7 oz
20	9	296 g	10.4 oz	343 g	12.1 oz
25	11	350 g	12.3 oz	405 g	14.3 oz
30	14	401 g	14.2 oz	464 g	16.4 oz
35	16	450 g	15.9 oz	521 g	18.4 oz
40	18	498 g	17.6 oz	576 g	20.3 oz
45	20	544 g	19.2 oz	629 g	22.2 oz
50	23	588 g	20.8 oz	681 g	24 oz
55	25	632 g	22.3 oz	732 g	25.8 oz
60	27	675 g	23.8 oz	781 g	27.6 oz
65	30	716 g	25.3 oz	829 g	29.3 oz
70	32	757 g	26.7 oz	877 g	31 oz
75	34	797 g	28.1 oz	923 g	32.6 oz
80	36	837 g	29.5 oz	969 g	34.2 oz
85	39	876 g	30.9 oz	1014 g	35.8 oz
90	41	914 g	32.3 oz	1059 g	37.3 oz
95	43	952 g	33.6 oz	1102 g	38.9 oz
100	45	989 g	34.9 oz	1146 g	40.4 oz

Pork, Duck and Brussels Sprouts

Protein: 60.8%, Fat: 20.2%, Carbohydrate: 12.9%, Minerals: 6.1% *(calculated based on dry matter)*

Total Calories: 1200 kcals *(1.5 kcals per gram or 42.3 kcals per ounce of food)*

Total Recipe Amount: 804g or 28.3oz

This meal is considered High Protein, Moderate Fat, Low Carb.

Ingredients:	Grams:	Ounces:
Ground pork, 96% lean, gently cooked	400 g	14.1 oz
Duck liver, raw	100 g	3.5 oz
Brussels sprouts, raw	100 g	3.5 oz
Sweet potato, gently cooked	60 g	2.1 oz
Spinach, boiled, drained, no salt	50 g	1.8 oz
Apples, raw, with skin, chopped	30 g	1.1 oz
Oysters, raw or canned in water	25 g	0.9 oz
Hempseed oil	18 g	0.6 oz
Egg yolk	15 g	0.5 oz
Egg shell powder	5 g	0.2 oz
Kelp, dried, I = 700 mcg/g	0.5 g	0.02 oz
Vitamin D drops, 100 IU/drop, 1 drop is 0.033g	0.033 g	1 drop

Cooking Instructions:

1. **Cook Ground Pork & Sweet Potato:** Add the ground pork and diced sweet potato to the slow cooker. Cook on low for 3 hours until the pork is fully cooked.

2. **Add Duck Liver & Oysters:** In the last 30 minutes, add the duck liver and oysters (raw or canned in water) to the slow cooker.

3. **Add Brussels Sprouts & Spinach:** During the last 15 minutes, stir in the brussels sprouts and boiled, drained spinach.

4. **Cool & Combine:** Once cooking is complete, turn off the slow cooker and allow the mixture to cool slightly. Stir in the chopped apples, hempseed oil, egg yolk, egg shell powder, and dried kelp.

5. **Add Vitamin D:** Once the mixture has cooled to room temperature, add the vitamin D drop.

6. **Stir & Blend:** Thoroughly mix all ingredients together to ensure even distribution.

7. **Portion & Store:** Portion into daily servings. Store in the fridge for 3 days or freeze for up to 1 month.

Daily Meal Portioning based on Dog's Weight:

Tip: If your dog eats two meals a day, divide the total daily amount of food in half and serve it across both meals.

Dog's Weight		Daily Meal Portion			
		Less Active Dog		Active Dog	
Pounds (lbs)	Kilograms (kgs)	Grams	Ounces	Grams	Ounces
5	2	118 g	4.2 oz	136 g	4.8 oz
10	5	198 g	7 oz	229 g	8.1 oz
15	7	268 g	9.5 oz	310 g	11 oz
20	9	333 g	11.7 oz	385 g	13.6 oz
25	11	393 g	13.9 oz	455 g	16.1 oz
30	14	451 g	15.9 oz	522 g	18.4 oz
35	16	506 g	17.9 oz	586 g	20.7 oz
40	18	560 g	19.7 oz	648 g	22.8 oz
45	20	611 g	21.6 oz	707 g	25 oz
50	23	661 g	23.3 oz	766 g	27 oz
55	25	710 g	25.1 oz	822 g	29 oz
60	27	758 g	26.7 oz	878 g	31 oz
65	30	805 g	28.4 oz	932 g	32.9 oz
70	32	851 g	30 oz	985 g	34.8 oz
75	34	896 g	31.6 oz	1038 g	36.6 oz
80	36	941 g	33.2 oz	1089 g	38.4 oz
85	39	984 g	34.7 oz	1140 g	40.2 oz
90	41	1028 g	36.2 oz	1190 g	42 oz
95	43	1070 g	37.8 oz	1239 g	43.7 oz
100	45	1112 g	39.2 oz	1288 g	45.4 oz

Pork, Oyster and Broccoli

Protein: 59.9%, Fat: 21.6%, Carbohydrate: 12%, Minerals: 6.5% (calculated based on dry matter)

Total Calories: 900 kcals (1.4 kcals per gram or 40.8 kcals per ounce of food)

Total Recipe Amount: 625g or 22.1oz

This meal is considered High Protein, Moderate Fat, Low Carb.

Ingredients:	Grams:	Ounces:
Ground pork, 96% lean, gently cooked	300 g	10.6 oz
Broccoli, gently cooked	100 g	3.5 oz
Oysters, raw or canned in water	85 g	3 oz
Oats, cooked, unenriched, no salt added	50 g	1.8 oz
Blueberries, raw	40 g	1.4 oz
Lamb liver, raw	20 g	0.7 oz
Hempseed oil	15 g	0.5 oz
Egg yolk	10 g	0.4 oz
Egg shell powder	5 g	0.2 oz
Kelp, dried, I = 700 mcg/g	0.2 g	0.01 oz
Vitamin D drops, 100 IU/drop, 1 drop is 0.033g	0.033 g	1 drop

Cooking Instructions:

1. **Cook Ground Pork & Broccoli:** Add the ground pork and broccoli to the slow cooker. Cook on low for 3 hours until the pork is fully cooked.

2. **Add Lamb Liver & Oysters:** In the last 30 minutes, add the lamb liver and oysters (raw or canned in water) to the slow cooker.

3. **Add Cooked Oats:** In the last 15 minutes of cooking, stir in the cooked oats.

4. **Cool & Combine:** Once cooking is complete, turn off the slow cooker and allow the mixture to cool slightly. Stir in blueberries, hempseed oil, egg yolk, egg shell powder, and dried kelp.

5. **Add Vitamin D:** Once the mixture has cooled to room temperature, add the vitamin D drop.

6. **Stir & Blend:** Thoroughly mix all ingredients together to ensure even distribution.

7. **Portion & Store:** Portion into daily servings. Store in the fridge for 3 days or freeze for up to 1 month.

Daily Meal Portioning based on Dog's Weight:

Tip: If your dog eats two meals a day, divide the total daily amount of food in half and serve it across both meals.

Dog's Weight		Daily Meal Portion			
		Less Active Dog		Active Dog	
Pounds (lbs)	Kilograms (kgs)	Grams	Ounces	Grams	Ounces
5	2	122 g	4.3 oz	141 g	5 oz
10	5	205 g	7.2 oz	237 g	8.4 oz
15	7	278 g	9.8 oz	322 g	11.4 oz
20	9	345 g	12.2 oz	399 g	14.1 oz
25	11	408 g	14.4 oz	472 g	16.7 oz
30	14	467 g	16.5 oz	541 g	19.1 oz
35	16	525 g	18.5 oz	608 g	21.4 oz
40	18	580 g	20.5 oz	672 g	23.7 oz
45	20	634 g	22.4 oz	734 g	25.9 oz
50	23	686 g	24.2 oz	794 g	28 oz
55	25	737 g	26 oz	853 g	30.1 oz
60	27	786 g	27.7 oz	910 g	32.1 oz
65	30	835 g	29.5 oz	967 g	34.1 oz
70	32	883 g	31.1 oz	1022 g	36 oz
75	34	929 g	32.8 oz	1076 g	38 oz
80	36	975 g	34.4 oz	1130 g	39.8 oz
85	39	1021 g	36 oz	1182 g	41.7 oz
90	41	1066 g	37.6 oz	1234 g	43.5 oz
95	43	1110 g	39.1 oz	1285 g	45.3 oz
100	45	1153 g	40.7 oz	1335 g	47.1 oz

Pork, Sardines and Green Beans

Protein: 59.9%, Fat: 27.8%, Carbohydrate: 6.3%, Minerals: 6% (calculated based on dry matter)

Total Calories: 1646 kcals (1.7 kcals per gram or 48 kcals per ounce of food)

Total Recipe Amount: 972g or 34.3oz

This meal is considered High Protein, Moderate Fat, Low Carb.

Ingredients:	Grams:	Ounces:
Ground pork, 96% lean, gently cooked	350 g	12.4 oz
Sardines, canned in water, no salt	300 g	10.6 oz
Green beans, raw	165 g	5.8 oz
Oysters, raw or canned in water	70 g	2.5 oz
Egg yolk	60 g	2.1 oz
Hempseed oil	18 g	0.6 oz
Egg shell powder	5 g	0.2 oz
Turmeric, ground	3 g	0.1 oz
Kelp, dried, I = 700 mcg/g	0.5 g	0.02 oz
Vitamin D drops, 100 IU/drop, 1 drop is 0.033g	0.033 g	1 drop

Cooking Instructions:

1. **Cook Ground Pork & Green Beans:** Add the ground pork and green beans to the slow cooker. Cook on low for 3 hours until the pork is fully cooked and the green beans are tender.

2. **Add Sardines & Oysters:** In the last 30 minutes, add the canned sardines (in water, no salt) and oysters (raw or canned in water) to the slow cooker.

3. **Add Egg Yolks:** During the last 15 minutes, stir in the egg yolks to the mixture.

4. **Cool & Combine:** Once cooking is complete, turn off the slow cooker and allow the mixture to cool slightly. Stir in hempseed oil, egg shell powder, ground turmeric, and dried kelp.

5. **Add Vitamin D:** Once the mixture has cooled to room temperature, add the vitamin D drop.

6. **Stir & Blend:** Thoroughly mix all ingredients together to ensure even distribution.

7. **Portion & Store:** Portion into daily servings. Store in the fridge for 3 days or freeze for up to 1 month.

Daily Meal Portioning based on Dog's Weight:

Tip: If your dog eats two meals a day, divide the total daily amount of food in half and serve it across both meals.

Dog's Weight		Daily Meal Portion			
		Less Active Dog		Active Dog	
Pounds (lbs)	Kilograms (kgs)	Grams	Ounces	Grams	Ounces
5	2	104 g	3.7 oz	120 g	4.2 oz
10	5	174 g	6.1 oz	202 g	7.1 oz
15	7	236 g	8.3 oz	274 g	9.7 oz
20	9	293 g	10.3 oz	339 g	12 oz
25	11	347 g	12.2 oz	401 g	14.2 oz
30	14	397 g	14 oz	460 g	16.2 oz
35	16	446 g	15.7 oz	516 g	18.2 oz
40	18	493 g	17.4 oz	571 g	20.1 oz
45	20	538 g	19 oz	623 g	22 oz
50	23	583 g	20.6 oz	675 g	23.8 oz
55	25	626 g	22.1 oz	725 g	25.6 oz
60	27	668 g	23.6 oz	774 g	27.3 oz
65	30	709 g	25 oz	821 g	29 oz
70	32	750 g	26.5 oz	868 g	30.6 oz
75	34	790 g	27.9 oz	914 g	32.3 oz
80	36	829 g	29.2 oz	960 g	33.9 oz
85	39	867 g	30.6 oz	1004 g	35.4 oz
90	41	905 g	31.9 oz	1048 g	37 oz
95	43	943 g	33.3 oz	1092 g	38.5 oz
100	45	980 g	34.6 oz	1135 g	40 oz

Pork, Salmon and Spinach

Protein: 66.9%, Fat: 22.3%, Carbohydrate: 3.6%, Minerals: 7.2% (calculated based on dry matter)

Total Calories: 913 kcals (1.6 kcals per gram or 45.2 kcals per ounce of food)

Total Recipe Amount: 572g or 20.2oz

This meal is considered High Protein, Moderate Fat, Low Carb.

Ingredients:	Grams:	Ounces:
Ground pork, 96% lean, gently cooked	300 g	10.6 oz
Salmon, gently cooked	80 g	2.8 oz
Spinach, boiled and drained, no salt	80 g	2.8 oz
Oysters, raw or canned in water	85 g	3 oz
Hempseed oil	12 g	0.4 oz
Egg yolk	10 g	0.4 oz
Egg shell powder	5 g	0.2 oz
Kelp, dried, I = 700 mcg/g	0.2 g	0.01 oz

Cooking Instructions:

1. **Cook Ground Pork & Salmon:** Add the ground pork and salmon to the slow cooker. Cook on low for 3 hours until the pork and salmon are fully cooked.

2. **Add Oysters & Spinach:** In the last 30 minutes, add the oysters (raw or canned in water) and the boiled, drained spinach to the slow cooker.

3. **Cool & Combine:** Once cooking is complete, turn off the slow cooker and allow the mixture to cool slightly. Stir in hempseed oil, egg yolk, egg shell powder, and dried kelp.

4. **Stir & Blend:** Thoroughly mix all ingredients together to ensure even distribution.

5. **Portion & Store:** Portion into daily servings. Store in the fridge for 3 days or freeze for up to 1 month.

Daily Meal Portioning based on Dog's Weight:

Tip: If your dog eats two meals a day, divide the total daily amount of food in half and serve it across both meals.

Dog's Weight		Daily Meal Portion			
		Less Active Dog		Active Dog	
Pounds (lbs)	Kilograms (kgs)	Grams	Ounces	Grams	Ounces
5	2	110 g	3.9 oz	127 g	4.5 oz
10	5	185 g	6.5 oz	214 g	7.6 oz
15	7	251 g	8.9 oz	291 g	10.3 oz
20	9	311 g	11 oz	361 g	12.7 oz
25	11	368 g	13 oz	426 g	15 oz
30	14	422 g	14.9 oz	489 g	17.2 oz
35	16	474 g	16.7 oz	548 g	19.3 oz
40	18	524 g	18.5 oz	606 g	21.4 oz
45	20	572 g	20.2 oz	662 g	23.4 oz
50	23	619 g	21.8 oz	717 g	25.3 oz
55	25	665 g	23.5 oz	770 g	27.2 oz
60	27	710 g	25 oz	822 g	29 oz
65	30	754 g	26.6 oz	872 g	30.8 oz
70	32	797 g	28.1 oz	922 g	32.5 oz
75	34	839 g	29.6 oz	971 g	34.3 oz
80	36	880 g	31.1 oz	1019 g	36 oz
85	39	921 g	32.5 oz	1067 g	37.6 oz
90	41	962 g	33.9 oz	1114 g	39.3 oz
95	43	1002 g	35.3 oz	1160 g	40.9 oz
100	45	1041 g	36.7 oz	1205 g	42.5 oz

Hypoallergenic Recipes: Alternative Meats

In the next section, you'll find recipes featuring venison, rabbit, bison, duck, and lamb which are ideal for dogs with food intolerances. These are alternative meats to traditional proteins like chicken, turkey, beef and pork.

Venison, Duck and Squash

Venison, a less common protein source, presents a lower risk of triggering food allergies or sensitivities in dogs. It is also lean, high in protein, and rich in essential nutrients like B vitamins, zinc, and iron, which support overall health and vitality.

Protein: 59.6%, Fat: 22.4%, Carbohydrate: 10.8%, Minerals: 7.2% *(calculated based on dry matter)*

Total Calories: 623 kcals *(1.3 kcals per gram or 36.9 kcals per ounce of food)*

Total Recipe Amount: 478g or 16.9oz

This meal is High Protein, Moderate Fat, Low Carb.

Ingredients:	Grams:	Ounces:
Ground venison, gently cooked	200 g	7.1 oz
Duck liver, raw	125 g	4.4 oz
Zucchini, includes skin, gently cooked	50 g	1.8 oz
Butternut squash, gently cooked	50 g	1.8 oz
Carrots, raw, grated	40 g	1.4 oz
Hempseed oil	8 g	0.3 oz
Egg shell powder	5 g	0.2 oz
Kelp, dried, I = 700 mcg/g	0.3 g	0.01 oz
Vitamin D drops, 100 IU/drop, 1 drop is 0.033g	0.033 g	1 drop

Cooking Instructions:

1. **Cook Ground Venison & Vegetables:** Add the ground venison, diced zucchini (with skin), and diced butternut squash to the slow cooker. Cook on low for 3 hours until the venison is fully cooked.

2. **Add Duck Liver:** In the last 30 minutes, add the duck liver to the slow cooker and cook until done.

3. **Add Carrots:** In the last 15 minutes, stir in the grated carrots.

4. **Cool & Combine:** Once cooking is complete, turn off the slow cooker and allow the mixture to cool slightly. Stir in hempseed oil, egg shell powder, and dried kelp.

5. **Add Vitamin D:** Once the mixture has cooled to room temperature, add the vitamin D drop.

6. **Stir & Blend:** Thoroughly mix all ingredients together to ensure even distribution.

7. **Portion & Store:** Portion into daily servings. Store in the fridge for 3 days or freeze for up to 1 month.

Daily Meal Portioning based on Dog's Weight:

Tip: If your dog eats two meals a day, divide the total daily amount of food in half and serve it across both meals.

Dog's Weight		Daily Meal Portion			
		Less Active Dog		Active Dog	
Pounds (lbs)	Kilograms (kgs)	Grams	Ounces	Grams	Ounces
5	2	135 g	4.8 oz	156 g	5.6 oz
10	5	227 g	8 oz	262 g	9.3 oz
15	7	307 g	10.8 oz	356 g	12.5 oz
20	9	381 g	13.4 oz	441 g	15.6 oz
25	11	451 g	15.9 oz	522 g	18.4 oz
30	14	517 g	18.2 oz	598 g	21.1 oz
35	16	580 g	20.5 oz	671 g	23.7 oz
40	18	641 g	22.6 oz	742 g	26.2 oz
45	20	700 g	24.7 oz	811 g	28.6 oz
50	23	758 g	26.7 oz	877 g	31 oz
55	25	814 g	28.7 oz	942 g	33.2 oz
60	27	869 g	30.6 oz	1006 g	35.5 oz
65	30	923 g	32.5 oz	1068 g	37.7 oz
70	32	975 g	34.4 oz	1129 g	39.8 oz
75	34	1027 g	36.2 oz	1189 g	42 oz
80	36	1078 g	38 oz	1248 g	44 oz
85	39	1128 g	39.8 oz	1306 g	46 oz
90	41	1178 g	41.5 oz	1363 g	48 oz
95	43	1226 g	43.3 oz	1420 g	50.1 oz
100	45	1274 g	45 oz	1476 g	52.1 oz

Venison, Oyster and Vegetables

Protein: 59.6%, Fat: 25%, Carbohydrate: 7.7%, Minerals: 7.7% (calculated based on dry matter)

Total Calories: 642 kcals (1.4 kcals per gram or 38.3 kcals per ounce of food)

Total Recipe Amount: 475g or 16.7oz

This meal is considered High Protein, Moderate Fat, Low Carb.

Ingredients:	Grams:	Ounces:
Ground venison, gently cooked	250 g	8.8 oz
Oysters, raw or canned in water	100 g	3.5 oz
Green beans, raw	55 g	1.9 oz
Zucchini, includes skin, gently cooked	55 g	1.9 oz
Hempseed oil	9 g	0.3 oz
Egg shell powder	5 g	0.2 oz
Kelp, dried, I = 700 mcg/g	0.5 g	0.02 oz
Vitamin D drops, 100 IU/drop, 1 drop is 0.033g	0.033 g	1 drop

Cooking Instructions:

1. **Cook Ground Venison & Zucchini:** Add the ground venison and diced zucchini (with skin) to the slow cooker. Cook on low for 3 hours until the venison is fully cooked.

2. **Add Oysters & Green Beans:** In the last 30 minutes, add the oysters (raw or canned in water) and green beans to the slow cooker.

3. **Cool & Combine:** Once cooking is complete, turn off the slow cooker and allow the mixture to cool slightly. Stir in hempseed oil, egg shell powder, and dried kelp.

4. **Add Vitamin D:** Once the mixture has cooled to room temperature, add the vitamin D drop.

5. **Stir & Blend:** Thoroughly mix all ingredients together to ensure even distribution.

6. **Portion & Store:** Portion into daily servings. Store in the fridge for 3 days or freeze for up to 1 month.

Daily Meal Portioning based on Dog's Weight:

Tip: If your dog eats two meals a day, divide the total daily amount of food in half and serve it across both meals.

Dog's Weight		Daily Meal Portion			
		Less Active Dog		Active Dog	
Pounds (lbs)	Kilograms (kgs)	Grams	Ounces	Grams	Ounces
5	2	130 g	4.6 oz	150 g	5.3 oz
10	5	218 g	7.7 oz	253 g	8.9 oz
15	7	296 g	10.4 oz	343 g	12.1 oz
20	9	367 g	13 oz	425 g	15 oz
25	11	434 g	15.3 oz	503 g	17.7 oz
30	14	498 g	17.6 oz	576 g	20.3 oz
35	16	559 g	19.7 oz	647 g	22.8 oz
40	18	618 g	21.8 oz	715 g	25.2 oz
45	20	675 g	23.8 oz	781 g	27.6 oz
50	23	730 g	25.8 oz	845 g	29.8 oz
55	25	784 g	27.7 oz	908 g	32 oz
60	27	837 g	29.5 oz	969 g	34.2 oz
65	30	889 g	31.4 oz	1030 g	36.3 oz
70	32	940 g	33.2 oz	1088 g	38.4 oz
75	34	990 g	34.9 oz	1146 g	40.4 oz
80	36	1039 g	36.6 oz	1203 g	42.4 oz
85	39	1087 g	38.3 oz	1259 g	44.4 oz
90	41	1135 g	40 oz	1314 g	46.4 oz
95	43	1182 g	41.7 oz	1368 g	48.3 oz
100	45	1228 g	43.3 oz	1422 g	50.2 oz

Lamb, Duck and Squash

Lamb is another excellent choice for dogs who are picky eaters or have allergies or sensitivities to poultry, such as chicken. It is also rich in high-quality protein, healthy fats, and essential nutrients like zinc and iron, which support overall health and immune function.

Protein: 52.2%, Fat: 30.2%, Carbohydrate: 11.6%, Minerals: 6% *(calculated based on dry matter)*

Total Calories: 1144 kcals *(1.5 kcals per gram or 41.2 kcals per ounce of food)*

Total Recipe Amount: 788g or 27.8oz

This meal is High Protein, Moderate Fat, Low Carb.

Ingredients:	Grams:	Ounces:
Ground lamb, gently cooked	300 g	10.6 oz
Duck liver, raw	200 g	7.1 oz
Zucchini, includes skin, gently cooked	100 g	3.5 oz
Butternut squash, gently cooked	100 g	3.5 oz
Carrots, raw, grated	80 g	2.8 oz
Egg shell powder	5 g	0.2 oz
Kelp, dried, I = 700 mcg/g	2.5 g	0.09 oz
Vitamin D drops, 100 IU/drop, 1 drop is 0.033g	0.033 g	1 drop
Vitamin E drops, 30 IU/drop, 1 drop is 0.033g	0.033 g	1 drop

Cooking Instructions:

1. **Cook Ground Lamb & Vegetables:** Add the ground lamb, diced zucchini (with skin), and diced butternut squash to the slow cooker. Cook on low for 3 hours until the lamb is fully cooked.

2. **Add Duck Liver:** In the last 30 minutes, add the duck liver to the slow cooker and cook until done.

3. **Add Carrots:** In the last 15 minutes, stir in the grated carrots.

4. **Cool & Combine:** Once cooking is complete, turn off the slow cooker and allow the mixture to cool slightly. Stir in egg shell powder and dried kelp.

5. **Add Vitamins:** Once the mixture has cooled to room temperature, add the drops of vitamin D and vitamin E.

6. **Stir & Blend:** Thoroughly mix all ingredients together to ensure even distribution.

7. **Portion & Store:** Portion into daily servings. Store in the fridge for 3 days or freeze for up to 1 month.

Daily Meal Portioning based on Dog's Weight:

Tip: If your dog eats two meals a day, divide the total daily amount of food in half and serve it across both meals.

Dog's Weight		Daily Meal Portion			
		Less Active Dog		Active Dog	
Pounds (lbs)	Kilograms (kgs)	Grams	Ounces	Grams	Ounces
5	2	121 g	4.3 oz	140 g	4.9 oz
10	5	203 g	7.2 oz	235 g	8.3 oz
15	7	276 g	9.7 oz	319 g	11.3 oz
20	9	342 g	12.1 oz	396 g	14 oz
25	11	404 g	14.3 oz	468 g	16.5 oz
30	14	463 g	16.3 oz	536 g	18.9 oz
35	16	520 g	18.4 oz	602 g	21.2 oz
40	18	575 g	20.3 oz	666 g	23.5 oz
45	20	628 g	22.1 oz	727 g	25.7 oz
50	23	680 g	24 oz	787 g	27.8 oz
55	25	730 g	25.8 oz	845 g	29.8 oz
60	27	779 g	27.5 oz	902 g	31.8 oz
65	30	827 g	29.2 oz	958 g	33.8 oz
70	32	875 g	30.9 oz	1013 g	35.7 oz
75	34	921 g	32.5 oz	1067 g	37.6 oz
80	36	967 g	34.1 oz	1120 g	39.5 oz
85	39	1012 g	35.7 oz	1172 g	41.3 oz
90	41	1056 g	37.3 oz	1223 g	43.1 oz
95	43	1100 g	38.8 oz	1273 g	44.9 oz
100	45	1143 g	40.3 oz	1324 g	46.7 oz

Duck, Oyster and Vegetables

Duck is an excellent alternative for dogs who have allergies because it is less common than chicken or beef, which are the most frequent causes of food allergies or sensitivities in dogs. It is also rich in protein, iron, and essential fatty acids, which help support skin, coat, and overall health.

Protein: 60%, Fat: 27%, Carbohydrate: 6.9%, Minerals: 6.1% *(calculated based on dry matter)*

Total Calories: 1148 kcals *(1.5 kcals per gram or 41.4 kcals per ounce of food)*

Total Recipe Amount: 785g or 27.8oz

This meal is High Protein, Moderate Fat, Low Carb.

Ingredients:	Grams:	Ounces:
Duck, gently cooked	300 g	10.6 oz
Duck liver, raw	290 g	10.2 oz
Zucchini, includes skin, gently cooked	50 g	1.8 oz
Spinach, boiled, drained, no salt	50 g	1.8 oz
Green beans, raw	50 g	1.8 oz
Oyster, raw or canned in water	20 g	0.7 oz
Hempseed oil	20 g	0.7 oz
Egg shell powder	5 g	0.2 oz
Kelp, dried, I = 700 mcg/g	0.4 g	0.01 oz
Vitamin D drops, 100 IU/drop, 1 drop is 0.033g	0.033 g	1 drop

Cooking Instructions:

1. **Cook Duck & Zucchini:** Add the duck meat and diced zucchini (with skin) to the slow cooker. Cook on low for 3 hours until the duck is fully cooked.

2. **Add Duck Liver & Oysters:** In the last 30 minutes, add the duck liver and oysters (raw or canned in water) to the slow cooker.

3. **Add Spinach & Green Beans:** During the last 15 minutes of cooking, stir in the boiled, drained spinach and green beans.

4. **Cool & Combine:** Once cooking is complete, turn off the slow cooker and allow the mixture to cool slightly. Stir in hempseed oil, egg shell powder, and dried kelp.

5. **Add Vitamin D:** Once the mixture has cooled to room temperature, add the vitamin D drop.

6. **Stir & Blend:** Thoroughly mix all ingredients together to ensure even distribution.

7. **Portion & Store:** Portion into daily servings. Store in the fridge for 3 days or freeze for up to 1 month.

Daily Meal Portioning based on Dog's Weight:

Tip: If your dog eats two meals a day, divide the total daily amount of food in half and serve it across both meals.

Dog's Weight		Daily Meal Portion			
		Less Active Dog		Active Dog	
Pounds (lbs)	Kilograms (kgs)	Grams	Ounces	Grams	Ounces
5	2	120 g	4.2 oz	139 g	4.9 oz
10	5	202 g	7.1 oz	234 g	8.3 oz
15	7	274 g	9.7 oz	317 g	11.2 oz
20	9	340 g	12 oz	393 g	13.9 oz
25	11	402 g	14.2 oz	465 g	16.4 oz
30	14	461 g	16.2 oz	533 g	18.8 oz
35	16	517 g	18.2 oz	599 g	21.1 oz
40	18	571 g	20.2 oz	662 g	23.3 oz
45	20	624 g	22 oz	723 g	25.5 oz
50	23	676 g	23.8 oz	782 g	27.6 oz
55	25	726 g	25.6 oz	840 g	29.6 oz
60	27	775 g	27.3 oz	897 g	31.6 oz
65	30	822 g	29 oz	952 g	33.6 oz
70	32	869 g	30.7 oz	1007 g	35.5 oz
75	34	916 g	32.3 oz	1060 g	37.4 oz
80	36	961 g	33.9 oz	1113 g	39.3 oz
85	39	1006 g	35.5 oz	1165 g	41.1 oz
90	41	1050 g	37 oz	1216 g	42.9 oz
95	43	1093 g	38.6 oz	1266 g	44.6 oz
100	45	1136 g	40.1 oz	1315 g	46.4 oz

Rabbit, Bison and Vegetables

Rabbit is a lean meat that is high in protein and low in fat, which can help dogs with weight management or digestive issues. This is another good novel protein for dogs as it is less likely to cause allergic reactions or sensitivities than chicken or beef, which are the most common proteins in dog food.

Protein: 65%, Fat: 16.4%, Carbohydrate: 11.8%, Minerals: 6.8% *(calculated based on dry matter)*

Total Calories: 999 kcals *(1.5 kcals per gram or 41.2 kcals per ounce of food)*

Total Recipe Amount: 687g or 24.2oz

This meal is High Protein, Low Fat, Low Carb.

Ingredients:	Grams:	Ounces:
Rabbit, gently cooked	300 g	10.6 oz
Bison liver, raw	200 g	7.1 oz
Zucchini, includes skin, gently cooked	50 g	1.8 oz
Spinach, boiled, drained, no salt	50 g	1.8 oz
Brown rice, cooked,	50 g	1.8 oz
Oysters, raw or canned in water	15 g	0.5 oz
Hempseed oil	15 g	0.5 oz
Egg shell powder	5 g	0.2 oz
Kelp, dried, I = 700 mcg/g	1.4 g	0.05 oz
Nutritional yeast	0.6 g	0.02 oz
Vitamin D drops, 100 IU/drop, 1 drop is 0.033g	0.033 g	1 drop

Cooking Instructions:

1. **Cook Rabbit & Zucchini:** Add the rabbit meat and diced zucchini (with skin) to the slow cooker. Cook on low for 3 hours until the rabbit is fully cooked.

2. **Add Bison Liver & Oysters:** In the last 30 minutes, add the bison liver and oysters (raw or canned in water) to the slow cooker.

3. **Add Spinach & Brown Rice:** During the last 15 minutes of cooking, stir in the boiled, drained spinach and cooked brown rice.

4. **Cool & Combine:** Once cooking is complete, turn off the slow cooker and allow the mixture to cool slightly. Stir in hempseed oil, egg shell powder, nutritional yeast, and dried kelp.

5. **Add Vitamin D:** Once the mixture has cooled to room temperature, add the vitamin D drop.

6. **Stir & Blend:** Thoroughly mix all ingredients together to ensure even distribution.

7. **Portion & Store:** Portion into daily servings. Store in the fridge for 3 days or freeze for up to 1 month.

Daily Meal Portioning based on Dog's Weight:

Tip: If your dog eats two meals a day, divide the total daily amount of food in half and serve it across both meals.

Dog's Weight		Daily Meal Portion			
		Less Active Dog		Active Dog	
Pounds (lbs)	Kilograms (kgs)	Grams	Ounces	Grams	Ounces
5	2	121 g	4.3 oz	140 g	4.9 oz
10	5	203 g	7.2 oz	235 g	8.3 oz
15	7	275 g	9.7 oz	319 g	11.2 oz
20	9	341 g	12 oz	395 g	13.9 oz
25	11	404 g	14.2 oz	467 g	16.5 oz
30	14	463 g	16.3 oz	536 g	18.9 oz
35	16	520 g	18.3 oz	602 g	21.2 oz
40	18	574 g	20.3 oz	665 g	23.5 oz
45	20	627 g	22.1 oz	726 g	25.6 oz
50	23	679 g	24 oz	786 g	27.7 oz
55	25	729 g	25.7 oz	844 g	29.8 oz
60	27	778 g	27.5 oz	901 g	31.8 oz
65	30	826 g	29.2 oz	957 g	33.8 oz
70	32	874 g	30.8 oz	1012 g	35.7 oz
75	34	920 g	32.5 oz	1065 g	37.6 oz
80	36	966 g	34.1 oz	1118 g	39.4 oz
85	39	1011 g	35.7 oz	1170 g	41.3 oz
90	41	1055 g	37.2 oz	1221 g	43.1 oz
95	43	1099 g	38.8 oz	1272 g	44.9 oz
100	45	1142 g	40.3 oz	1322 g	46.6 oz

Bison, Spinach and Green Beans

Bison is an excellent alternative for dogs with food allergies because it is a novel protein, meaning dogs are less likely to have been exposed to it, reducing the risk of allergic reactions. It is also lean, high in protein, and packed with essential nutrients like omega-3 fatty acids, iron, and zinc, which support overall health.

Protein: 67%, Fat: 16.8%, Carbohydrate: 11.1%, Minerals: 5.1% *(calculated based on dry matter)*

Total Calories: 1010 kcals *(1.4 kcals per gram or 39.7 kcals per ounce of food)*

Total Recipe Amount: 722g or 25.5oz

This meal is High Protein, Low Fat, Low Carb.

Ingredients:	Grams:	Ounces:
Bison, gently cooked	300 g	10.6 oz
Bison liver, raw	300 g	10.6 oz
Green beans, raw	50 g	1.8 oz
Spinach, boiled and drained, no salt	50 g	1.8 oz
Hempseed oil	15 g	0.5 oz
Egg shell powder	5 g	0.2 oz
Kelp, dried, I = 700 mcg/g	1.5 g	0.05 oz
Nutritional yeast	0.5 g	0.02 oz
Vitamin D drops, 100 IU/drop, 1 drop is 0.033g	0.033 g	1 drop

Cooking Instructions:

1. **Cook Bison & Green Beans:** Add the bison meat and green beans to the slow cooker. Cook on low for 3 hours until the bison is fully cooked.

2. **Add Bison Liver:** In the last 30 minutes, add the bison liver to the slow cooker and cook until done.

3. **Add Spinach:** During the last 15 minutes, stir in the boiled, drained spinach.

4. **Cool & Combine:** Once cooking is complete, turn off the slow cooker and allow the mixture to cool slightly. Stir in hempseed oil, egg shell powder, nutritional yeast, and dried kelp.

5. **Add Vitamin D:** Once the mixture has cooled to room temperature, add the vitamin D drop.

6. **Stir & Blend:** Thoroughly mix all ingredients together to ensure even distribution.

7. **Portion & Store:** Portion into daily servings. Store in the fridge for 3 days or freeze for up to 1 month.

Daily Meal Portioning based on Dog's Weight:

Tip: If your dog eats two meals a day, divide the total daily amount of food in half and serve it across both meals.

Dog's Weight		Daily Meal Portion			
		Less Active Dog		Active Dog	
Pounds (lbs)	Kilograms (kgs)	Grams	Ounces	Grams	Ounces
5	2	125 g	4.4 oz	145 g	5.1 oz
10	5	211 g	7.4 oz	244 g	8.6 oz
15	7	286 g	10.1 oz	331 g	11.7 oz
20	9	355 g	12.5 oz	411 g	14.5 oz
25	11	419 g	14.8 oz	486 g	17.1 oz
30	14	481 g	17 oz	557 g	19.6 oz
35	16	540 g	19 oz	625 g	22.1 oz
40	18	597 g	21.1 oz	691 g	24.4 oz
45	20	652 g	23 oz	755 g	26.6 oz
50	23	705 g	24.9 oz	817 g	28.8 oz
55	25	758 g	26.7 oz	877 g	31 oz
60	27	809 g	28.5 oz	937 g	33 oz
65	30	859 g	30.3 oz	994 g	35.1 oz
70	32	908 g	32 oz	1051 g	37.1 oz
75	34	956 g	33.7 oz	1107 g	39 oz
80	36	1004 g	35.4 oz	1162 g	41 oz
85	39	1050 g	37.1 oz	1216 g	42.9 oz
90	41	1096 g	38.7 oz	1269 g	44.8 oz
95	43	1142 g	40.3 oz	1322 g	46.6 oz
100	45	1186 g	41.9 oz	1374 g	48.5 oz

Hypoallergenic Recipes: Fish

Fish, often a new protein source for many dogs, is rich in naturally present omega-3 fatty acids. These fatty acids are known to aid dogs suffering from various allergies. Therefore, if a dog has both food and seasonal allergies, incorporating fish into their diet could potentially address both problems, enhancing their overall well-being.

Catfish, Sardines and Oyster

Protein: 57%, Fat: 25%, Carbohydrate: 9.5%, Minerals: 8.5% *(calculated based on dry matter)*

Total Calories: 753 kcals *(1.2 kcals per gram or 33.3 kcals per ounce of food)*

Total Recipe Amount: 640g or 22.6oz

This meal is High Protein, Moderate Fat, Low Carb.

Ingredients:	Grams:	Ounces:
Catfish, gently cooked	250 g	8.8 oz
Sardines, canned in water, no salt	100 g	3.5 oz
Oysters, raw or canned in water	100 g	3.5 oz
Mussels, raw or canned	50 g	1.8 oz
Zucchini, includes skin, gently cooked	50 g	1.8 oz
Apples, raw, with skin, chopped	50 g	1.8 oz
Egg yolk	25 g	0.9 oz
Hempseed oil	10 g	0.4 oz
Egg shell powder	5 g	0.2 oz
Nutritional yeast	0.4 g	0.01 oz

Cooking Instructions:

1. **Cook Catfish & Zucchini:** Add the catfish and diced zucchini (with skin) to the slow cooker. Cook on low for 2-3 hours until the catfish is fully cooked.

2. **Add Sardines, Oysters, & Mussels:** In the last 30 minutes, add the canned sardines (in water, no salt), raw or canned oysters, and raw or canned mussels to the slow cooker.

3. **Add Apples:** In the last 15 minutes, stir in the chopped apples (with skin).

4. **Cool & Combine:** Once cooking is complete, turn off the slow cooker and allow the mixture to cool slightly. Stir in egg yolk, hempseed oil, egg shell powder, and nutritional yeast.

5. **Stir & Blend:** Thoroughly mix all ingredients together to ensure even distribution.

6. **Portion & Store:** Portion into daily servings. Store in the fridge for 3 days or freeze for up to 1 month.

Daily Meal Portioning based on Dog's Weight:

Tip: If your dog eats two meals a day, divide the total daily amount of food in half and serve it across both meals.

Dog's Weight		Daily Meal Portion			
		Less Active Dog		Active Dog	
Pounds (lbs)	Kilograms (kgs)	Grams	Ounces	Grams	Ounces
5	2	149 g	5.3 oz	173 g	6.1 oz
10	5	251 g	8.9 oz	291 g	10.3 oz
15	7	340 g	12 oz	394 g	13.9 oz
20	9	422 g	14.9 oz	489 g	17.3 oz
25	11	499 g	17.6 oz	578 g	20.4 oz
30	14	572 g	20.2 oz	663 g	23.4 oz
35	16	643 g	22.7 oz	744 g	26.3 oz
40	18	710 g	25.1 oz	822 g	29 oz
45	20	776 g	27.4 oz	898 g	31.7 oz
50	23	840 g	29.6 oz	972 g	34.3 oz
55	25	902 g	31.8 oz	1044 g	36.8 oz
60	27	963 g	34 oz	1115 g	39.3 oz
65	30	1022 g	36 oz	1184 g	41.8 oz
70	32	1081 g	38 oz	1251 g	44.1 oz
75	34	1138 g	40.2 oz	1318 g	46.5 oz
80	36	1195 g	42.1 oz	1383 g	48.8 oz
85	39	1250 g	44.1 oz	1448 g	51.1 oz
90	41	1305 g	46 oz	1511 g	53.3 oz
95	43	1359 g	47.9 oz	1574 g	55.5 oz
100	45	1412 g	49.8 oz	1635 g	57.7 oz

Cod, Salmon and Pumpkin

Protein: 71.1%, Fat: 15.8%, Carbohydrate: 3.9%, Minerals: 9.2% *(calculated based on dry matter)*

Total Calories: 613 kcals *(1 kcals per gram or 28.7 kcals per ounce of food)*

Total Recipe Amount: 606g or 21.4oz

This meal is High Protein, Low Fat, Low Carb.

Ingredients:	Grams:	Ounces:
Atlantic cod, gently cooked	300 g	10.6 oz
Salmon, gently cooked	100 g	3.5 oz
Pumpkin, canned, without salt	60 g	2.1 oz
Oysters, raw or canned in water	50 g	1.8 oz
Tomatoes, raw	40 g	1.4 oz
Spinach, boiled, drained, no salt	40 g	1.4 oz
Hempseed oil	10 g	0.4 oz
Egg shell powder	5 g	0.2 oz
Nutritional yeast	0.5 g	0.02 oz

Cooking Instructions:

1. **Cook Cod & Salmon:** Add the Atlantic cod and salmon to the slow cooker. Cook on low for 2-3 hours until both are fully cooked.

2. **Add Oysters & Spinach:** In the last 30 minutes, add the oysters (raw or canned in water) and boiled, drained spinach.

3. **Add Tomatoes & Pumpkin:** In the last 15 minutes, stir in the tomatoes and canned 100% pure pumpkin.

4. **Cool & Combine:** Once cooking is complete, turn off the slow cooker and allow the mixture to cool slightly. Stir in hempseed oil, egg shell powder, and nutritional yeast.

5. **Stir & Blend:** Thoroughly mix all ingredients together to ensure even distribution.

6. **Portion & Store:** Portion into daily servings. Store in the fridge for 3 days or freeze for up to 1 month.

Daily Meal Portioning based on Dog's Weight:

Tip: If your dog eats two meals a day, divide the total daily amount of food in half and serve it across both meals.

Dog's Weight		Daily Meal Portion			
		Less Active Dog		Active Dog	
Pounds (lbs)	Kilograms (kgs)	Grams	Ounces	Grams	Ounces
5	2	173 g	6.1 oz	201 g	7.1 oz
10	5	292 g	10.3 oz	338 g	12 oz
15	7	395 g	14 oz	458 g	16.1 oz
20	9	491 g	17.3 oz	568 g	20.1 oz
25	11	580 g	20.5 oz	672 g	23.7 oz
30	14	665 g	23.5 oz	770 g	27.2 oz
35	16	747 g	26.3 oz	864 g	30.5 oz
40	18	825 g	29.1 oz	955 g	33.7 oz
45	20	901 g	31.8 oz	1044 g	36.8 oz
50	23	975 g	34.4 oz	1129 g	39.9 oz
55	25	1048 g	37 oz	1213 g	42.8 oz
60	27	1118 g	39.5 oz	1295 g	45.7 oz
65	30	1187 g	41.9 oz	1375 g	48.5 oz
70	32	1255 g	44.3 oz	1454 g	51.3 oz
75	34	1322 g	46.6 oz	1531 g	54 oz
80	36	1388 g	49 oz	1607 g	56.7 oz
85	39	1452 g	51.2 oz	1681 g	59.3 oz
90	41	1516 g	53.5 oz	1755 g	62 oz
95	43	1579 g	55.7 oz	1828 g	64.5 oz
100	45	1640 g	57.9 oz	1899 g	67 oz

Sardines, Oyster and Spinach

Protein: 50.2%, Fat: 29.3%, Carbohydrate: 9.2%, Minerals: 11.3% *(calculated based on dry matter)*

Total Calories: 506 kcals *(1.2 kcals per gram or 33.6 kcals per ounce of food)*

Total Recipe Amount: 426g or 15oz

This meal is High Protein, Moderate Fat, and Low Carb.

Ingredients:	Grams:	Ounces:
Sardines, canned in water, no salt	125 g	4.4 oz
Oysters, raw or canned in water	125 g	4.4 oz
Spinach, boiled, drained, no salt	60 g	2.1 oz
Tomatoes, red, ripe, raw	60 g	2.1 oz
Salmon, gently cooked	35 g	1.2 oz
Egg yolk	8 g	0.3 oz
Hempseed oil	8 g	0.3 oz
Egg shell powder	5 g	0.2 oz
Nutritional yeast	0.3 g	0.01 oz

Cooking Instructions:

1. **Cook Salmon:** Add the salmon to the slow cooker. Cook on low for 2-3 hours until fully cooked.

2. **Add Sardines & Oysters:** In the last 30 minutes, add the canned sardines (in water, no salt) and oysters (raw or canned in water) to the slow cooker.

3. **Add Spinach & Tomatoes:** In the last 15 minutes, stir in the boiled, drained spinach and chopped tomatoes.

4. **Cool & Combine:** Once cooking is complete, turn off the slow cooker and allow the mixture to cool slightly. Stir in egg yolk, hempseed oil, egg shell powder, and nutritional yeast.

5. **Stir & Blend:** Thoroughly mix all ingredients together to ensure even distribution.

6. **Portion & Store:** Portion into daily servings. Store in the fridge for 3 days or freeze for up to 1 month.

Daily Meal Portioning based on Dog's Weight:

Tip: If your dog eats two meals a day, divide the total daily amount of food in half and serve it across both meals.

Dog's Weight		Daily Meal Portion			
Pounds (lbs)	Kilograms (kgs)	Less Active Dog		Active Dog	
		Grams	Ounces	Grams	Ounces
5	2	148 g	5.2 oz	171 g	6 oz
10	5	249 g	8.8 oz	288 g	10.2 oz
15	7	337 g	11.9 oz	391 g	13.8 oz
20	9	418 g	14.8 oz	485 g	17.1 oz
25	11	495 g	17.5 oz	573 g	20.2 oz
30	14	567 g	20 oz	657 g	23.2 oz
35	16	637 g	22.5 oz	737 g	26 oz
40	18	704 g	24.8 oz	815 g	28.7 oz
45	20	769 g	27.1 oz	890 g	31.4 oz
50	23	832 g	29.3 oz	963 g	34 oz
55	25	894 g	31.5 oz	1035 g	36.5 oz
60	27	954 g	33.6 oz	1104 g	39 oz
65	30	1013 g	35.7 oz	1173 g	41.4 oz
70	32	1071 g	37.8 oz	1240 g	43.7 oz
75	34	1128 g	39.8 oz	1306 g	46.1 oz
80	36	1184 g	41.8 oz	1370 g	48.3 oz
85	39	1239 g	43.7 oz	1434 g	50.6 oz
90	41	1293 g	45.6 oz	1497 g	52.8 oz
95	43	1346 g	47.5 oz	1559 g	55 oz
100	45	1399 g	49.4 oz	1620 g	57.1 oz

Cod, Salmon and Broccoli

Protein: 69.7%, Fat: 9.1%, Carbohydrate: 12.5%, Minerals: 8.7% *(calculated based on dry matter)*

Total Calories: 638 kcals *(0.9 kcals per gram or 26.4 kcals per ounce of food)*

Total Recipe Amount: 686g or 24.2oz

This meal is High Protein, Low Fat, Low Carb.

Ingredients:	Grams:	Ounces:
Atlantic cod, gently cooked	400 g	14.1 oz
Broccoli, gently cooked	80 g	2.8 oz
Salmon, gently cooked	60 g	2.1 oz
Carrots, raw, grated	50 g	1.8 oz
Sweet potato, gently cooked	50 g	1.8 oz
Oysters, raw or canned in water	30 g	1.1 oz
Egg shell powder	5 g	0.2 oz
Hempseed oil	5 g	0.2 oz
Turmeric, ground	5 g	0.2 oz
Nutritional yeast	0.5 g	0.02 oz

Cooking Instructions:

1. **Cook Cod & Sweet Potato:** Add the Atlantic cod and diced sweet potato to the slow cooker. Cook on low for 2-3 hours until the cod is fully cooked.

2. **Add Salmon & Oysters:** In the last 30 minutes, add the salmon and oysters (raw or canned in water) to the slow cooker.

3. **Add Broccoli & Carrots:** In the last 15 minutes, stir in the broccoli and grated carrots.

4. **Cool & Combine:** Once cooking is complete, turn off the slow cooker and allow the mixture to cool slightly. Stir in hempseed oil, egg shell powder, ground turmeric, and nutritional yeast.

5. **Stir & Blend:** Thoroughly mix all ingredients together to ensure even distribution.

6. **Portion & Store:** Portion into daily servings. Store in the fridge for 3 days or freeze for up to 1 month.

Daily Meal Portioning based on Dog's Weight:

Tip: If your dog eats two meals a day, divide the total daily amount of food in half and serve it across both meals.

Dog's Weight		Daily Meal Portion			
Pounds (lbs)	Kilograms (kgs)	Less Active Dog		Active Dog	
		Grams	Ounces	Grams	Ounces
5	2	189 g	6.7 oz	218 g	7.7 oz
10	5	317 g	11.2 oz	367 g	13 oz
15	7	430 g	15.2 oz	498 g	17.6 oz
20	9	533 g	18.8 oz	618 g	21.8 oz
25	11	630 g	22.2 oz	730 g	25.8 oz
30	14	723 g	25.5 oz	837 g	29.5 oz
35	16	811 g	28.6 oz	940 g	33 oz
40	18	897 g	31.6 oz	1039 g	36.6 oz
45	20	980 g	34.6 oz	1134 g	40 oz
50	23	1060 g	37.4 oz	1227 g	43 oz
55	25	1139 g	40.2 oz	1319 g	46.5 oz
60	27	1216 g	42.9 oz	1408 g	49.7 oz
65	30	1291 g	45.6 oz	1495 g	52.7 oz
70	32	1365 g	48.1 oz	1580 g	55.8 oz
75	34	1437 g	50.7 oz	1664 g	58.7 oz
80	36	1508 g	53.2 oz	1747 g	61.6 oz
85	39	1579 g	55.7 oz	1828 g	64.5 oz
90	41	1648 g	58.1 oz	1908 g	67.3 oz
95	43	1716 g	60.5 oz	1987 g	70.1 oz
100	45	1783 g	62.9 oz	2065 g	72.8 oz

Conclusion

A S WE TURN THE final pages of this comprehensive homemade dog food guide, it's time to pause and reflect on the invaluable journey we've embarked upon together. This isn't just the end of a book; it's the beginning of a transformative adventure in canine nutrition and care. You've been equipped not only with a plethora of recipes, but also with the knowledge and understanding of what truly constitutes a healthy, balanced diet for your beloved pet.

Throughout this guide, we've delved deep into the essential nutrients required for your dog's well-being, exploring the critical roles of proteins, fats and complex carbohydrates. You've learned the significance of vitamins and minerals, and how to seamlessly transition your dog from commercial kibble to nourishing, home-cooked meals. This journey has been about more than just feeding your dog. It's been about understanding their unique dietary needs and preferences, crafting meals that cater to them, while prioritizing their health and happiness.

Remember, canine nutrition is ever-evolving. As new research emerges and our understanding deepens, it becomes imperative to stay informed and adapt our cooking techniques accordingly. Always consult with your veterinarian, especially when introducing significant dietary changes or addressing health concerns.

Each recipe in this guide is a starting point, a canvas for you to tailor to the unique tastes and nutritional requirements of your dog. Observing their reactions to different foods and adjusting their diet is part of this ongoing, loving process.

Now, armed with the knowledge of canine nutrition, the understanding of healthy ingredients, and a collection of complete and balanced recipes, the time has come for you to take the reins. You have the power to make a profound impact on your dog's health and happiness. Embrace this opportunity with enthusiasm and creativity.

So, as we close this book, remember: the journey doesn't end here. It's just the beginning of a healthier, happier life for your furry friend. Take these lessons, apply them with love, and watch as your dog thrives on the meals you lovingly prepare. Let's raise a toast to a future of joyous, healthy mealtimes with our canine companions. Here's to their health, happiness, and the many tail-wagging moments ahead!

Message from Ava Barkley

If you haven't already, it would mean the world to me if you could spare a moment to share your thoughts with a review on Amazon.

I make sure to read every review because your input is crucial to me. It helps me identify what aspects you enjoyed and what areas I can improve to better serve you and your dogs in my future books!

To leave a review, simply scan the QR code below (that matches the country you are in) with your phone camera to be taken to the book's review page.

UNITED STATES   CANADA   UNITED KINGDOM

If you prefer, you can also leave a review by:

1. Visiting the book's page on Amazon or locating it through your purchases.

2. Scrolling down to the bottom of the page and clicking on the "Write a Customer Review" button.

3. Leaving a star rating out of 5, or if you're feeling inspired, writing a short review to share your experience.

Thank you once more for your exceptional support. It is invaluable to me and to the countless dogs whose lives we are enhancing together.

References

AKC Staff. (2021, March 7). "Types of Dog Allergies and How to Treat Them." *American Kennel Club*. https://www.akc.org/expert-advice/health/dog-allergies-symptoms-treatment/

AKC Staff. (2022, March 02). "How to Switch & Transition Dog Foods." *American Kennel Club*. https://www.akc.org/expert-advice/nutrition/right-way-switch-dog-foods/

Bietz D. et al (2006). "Your Dog's Nutritional Needs: A Science-Based Guide for Dog Owners." *National Academy of Sciences.*

Brahlek, A. (2022, July, 21). "A Practical Guide for Dog Elimination Diets." *Grubbly Farms.* https://grubblyfarms.com/blogs/the-flyer/guide-for-dog-elimination-diets#:~:text=For%20a%20strict%20elimination%20diet,to%20the%20protein%20or%20carb

Canine Bible (2022, November 17). "10 Best Vet-Approved Home-made Dog Food Recipes: Nutritionally Complete, Easy & Cheap." *Canine Bible*. https://www.caninebible.com/homemade-dog-food-recipes/#Why-Feed-Homemade-Dog-Food

Caplan, C (n.d.). "The Top 7 Most Common Food Allergens for Dogs." *The Dog People.* https://www.rover.com/blog/7-common-food-allergens-dogs/#:~:text=Essenti

ally%2C%20they%20inherit%20the%20allergy,pork%2C%20rabbit%2C%20and
%20%EF%AC%81sh

Coates, J. (2020, February 10). "How to Tell if Your Dog Has Food Allergies."
PetMD. https://www.petmd.com/dog/nutrition/how-tell-if-your-dog-has-foo
d-allergies

Cosgrove, N. (2023, September 20). "How to Read Pet Food Labels & Ingredient
Lists (With Calorie Calculator)." *Pet Keen.* https://petkeen.com/read-pet-food
-labels-ingredient-lists/Reisen, J. (2020, November 4). How to Read a Dog Food
Label. *American Kennel Club.* https://www.akc.org/expert-advice/nutrition/h
ow-to-read-a-dog-food-label/

Dog Child (2023, January 24). "Science Backed Benefits of Home Cooking for
you Dog." *Dog Child.* https://dogchild.co/en-us/blogs/learn/science-backed-b
enefits-of-home-cooking-for-your-dog

Downs, A. (2022, April 22). "30 Pros, Cons, and Myths About Homemade Dog
Foods." *Top Dog Tips.* https://topdogtips.com/homemade-dog-food-recipes-p
ros-cons/

Flower, A (2022, August 20). "The Facts about Dog Nutrition." *Web MD.*
https://www.webmd.com/pets/dogs/dog-nutrition

Ginger and Friends. (n.d.). "Benefits of Homemade Dog Food - Why Homemade
Dog Food?" *Ginger and Friends.* https://gingercavalier.com/blog/benefits-of-h
omemade-dog-food-why-homemade-dog-food/#Money-Saving

Giovanelli, N. (2022b, January 25). "Dog food meal prep 101." *The Canine
Health Nut.* https://thecaninehealthnut.com/how-to-meal-prep-for-dogs

Giovanelli, N. (2022). "Home Cooked Dog Food Recipe Book" *The Canine
Health Nut.*

Jones, S (2023). "Best Homemade Dog Food Recipes: 7 Vet-Approved and Nutritionally Complete." *Canine Journal.* https://www.caninejournal.com/home
made-dog-food-recipes/

Kafka's Organic. (2020, November 28). "A comprehensive guide to supplements for dogs." *Kafka's Organics.* https://kafkasorganic.com/blogs/news/a-comprehensive-guide-to-supplements-for-dogs

Klien, J. (2016, May 24). "How to Tell If Your Dog Has Food Allergies." *American Kennel Club.* https://www.akc.org/expert-advice/nutrition/tell-if-dog-has-allergies/

Milne, T (2022, July 7). "The Pros and Cons of Kibble Dog Food (Good and Bad ingredients)." *For the Love of Dogs.* https://dogfriendlyscene.co.uk/the-pros-and-cons-of-kibble-dog-food/#Pros

Mmaennche. (2021, March 1). "How much water should a dog drink?" *Advanced Care Veterinary Hospital.* https://advancedpetvet.com/2021/02/16/how-much-water-should-a-dog-drink/

Nikki. (n.d.). "How to Transition Your Dog Onto a Fresh Food Diet." *The Canine Health Nut.* https://thecaninehealthnut.com/transitiondogtonewfood/

Primovic, D. (2015, September 8). "How to calculate your dog's Daily Calorie Intake." *How to Calculate Your Dog's Daily Calorie Intake.* https://www.petplace.com/article/dogs/pet-health/how-to-calculate-your-dogs-daily-calorie-intake

Pipin, G. (n.d.). "The Importance of Dog Nutrition." *The Canine Nutritionist.* https://www.caninenutritionist.co.uk/dog-nutrition/importance-of-dog-nutrition/

Quinn, L. (2019, December 17). "First study on human-grade dog food says whole, fresh food is highly digestible." *College of Agricultural, Consumer and Environmental Studies | University of Illinois.* https://aces.illinois.edu/news/first-study-human-grade-dog-food-says-whole-fresh-food-highly-digestible

Randall, S. (2023, July 20). "Switching to Homemade Dog Food Diet: 3 Things to Know." *Top Dog Tips.* https://topdogtips.com/before-switching-to-homemade-dog-food/

Stratton, M (2023, March 17). "Is Kibble Really Bad for Dogs? The Pros and Cons." *Pet Spruce.* https://petspruce.com/kibble-bad-dogs/

Stregowski, J. (2022, October 19). "Vet-Approved Homemade Dog Food Recipes." *The Spruce Pets.* https://www.thesprucepets.com/homemade-dog-food-recipes-5200240

Tupler, T (2021, February 1). "Dog Nutrition: Guide to Dog Food Nutrients." *Pet MD.* https://www.petmd.com/dog/nutrition/evr_dg_whats_in_a_balanced_dog_food#what%20goes%20into

Wag (n.d.). "How to Read Dog Food labels: A Guide for New Dog Owners." *The Daily Wag.* https://wagwalking.com/daily/read-dog-food-labels

Wimble, C. (2022, January 17). "Dangers of Processed Dog Food | Dog Nutrition Lessons | Ep. 2." *The Dog Nutritionist.* . https://www.youtube.com/watch?v=mkNWHk5AFcI. You Tube.

Wimble, C. (2022, January 18). "Why your fussy dog won't eat, and what to do! | Dog Nutrition Lessons | Ep. 17." *The Dog Nutritionist.* . https://www.youtube.com/watch?v=FViucq7LkeA&list=PL1aRQuLPBnbXWx_RYLOruwkvb_voPILSU&index=20. You Tube.

Wimble, C. (2023, August 3). "Homemade Dog Food Recipe - Itchy Skin." *The Dog Nutritionist.* https://www.youtube.com/watch?v=mae95YNJynE You Tube

Wimble, C. (2022). "The Nutrition Guide: Digital Edition 2022" *The Dog Nutritionist.*

Witter, L (2021, December 18). "Is Kibble Safe for Dogs." *Vet Help Direct.* https://vethelpdirect.com/vetblog/2021/12/18/is-kibble-safe-for-dogs/#h-pros-to-feeding-kibble

Image Credits: Shutterstock.com

Made in United States
Troutdale, OR
11/14/2024

24809598R00110